RESEARCH LIBRARY
OF
COLONIAL AMERICANA

CHURCH COVENANT

Two Tracts

ARNO PRESS

A New York Times Company

New York – 1972

Reprint Edition 1972 by Arno Press Inc.

Reprinted from copies in The Union Theological
Seminary Library

LC# 75-141115
ISBN 0-405-03329-X

Research Library of Colonial Americana
ISBN for complete set: 0-405-03270-6
See last pages of this volume for titles.

Manufactured in the United States of America

CONTENTS

Church-Government
AND
Church-Covenant
DISCVSSED,

In an Anſwer of the Elders of the ſeve-
rall Churches in
NEW-ENGLAND
To two and thirty Queſtions, ſent over
to them by divers Miniſters in *England*, to declare their judgments therein.

Together with an Apologie of the ſaid Elders in
New-England for Church-Covenant, ſent over
in Anſwer to Maſter *Bernard* in the
yeare 1639.

As alſo in an Anſwer to nine Poſitions about Church-
Government.

And now publiſhed for the ſatisfaction of all who deſire
reſolution in thoſe points.

LONDON,
Printed by *R.O.* and *G.D.* for *Benjamin Allen,*
Anno Dom. 1643.

To the
READER.

IT is not hard to believe that such discourses as this wil meet with divers censures, the prophane and ignorant loathing Christ, and any thing concerning him; the Formalist accounting such truths troublesom that may ingage him in the change of his opinions and practises, and some of the wisest will be apt to question the tyming such light as this : yea doubtles this pamphlet-glutted age will so looke upon it, and lay it by.

But because I doe conceive that this sword will not be sheath'd which is now drawn, till Church-work be better known, and more countenanced, and since safety is laid up in the Temple, Psa. 27. 3,4,5. I could not but help on this, which attended and practised may prove our security next to Christ. These were either sudden answers to our doubting and inquiring Brethren, or some satisfaction rendred about our so much slighted Church-Covenant, which wee could not but thinke might come to view, for the present stay to some faithfull soules, that call for light, and intend to use it well : for others, of what kind soever, we must leave their harder thoughts, among those usuall loads of scandals, that men of our judgement must carry, especially if zeale for the Truth draw them forth to publike observation; nor doe we purpose (God helping us) to succumbe under calumny, being the livery of quieter times then these , let us bee viler still, so God and his Arke may be more glorious. Yet this I doe professe for my selfe and Brethren that as we have not bin dealt with, nor convinc'd of any offence, so we shall ever be ready to give an account of that hope which is in us, being call'd thereunto; in the meane time we over looke these barkings of black mouthes, and wish a good Comment be made upon the text of our plaine meaning.

The onely way I know to reach Gods mind in Worship will bee to love the truth for it's owne sake : yea to love it when it shall condemne our practises and persons also : Who hath not observed that the first step to error is the declining the truth in love to it ?

*

Hence

Hence Popery begat her first brat, and hath nurst it up with the same milke; we would earnestly desire that none would call that unseasonable or unreasonable, which God seems even now to call for, at the calling of this Synode, and will carry so much Reason with it, as God and his truth will owne: more tendernes and respect to our Brethren we know not how to shew, who sent us these 32. Questions: no other dealing would we have from our brethren not consenting with us. Some Rivers have bin noted to differ in the colours of the water, yet running in the same Channell: let Jesus Christ be lifted up by us all; let us love him whil'st wee dispute about him.

Presbytery and Independency (as it is call'd) are the wayes of Worship and Church fellowship, now looked at, since (we hope) Episcopacy is Coffind out, and will be buried without expectation of another resurrection. We are much charged with what we own not, viz: Independency, when as we know not any Churches Reformed, more looking at sister Churches for helpe then ours doe, onely we cannot have rule yet discovered from any friend or enemy, that we should be under Canon, or power of any other Church; under their Councell we are. We need not tell the wise whence Tyranny grew in Churches, and how common wealths got their pressure in the like kind.

These be our sighs and hearty wishes, that selfe may be conquered in this poore Nation, which shuts the doore against these truths. Know (good Reader) we do not hereby go about to whistle thee out of any knowne good way of God. Commonly Questions and Answers cleare up the way, when other Treatises leave us to darknes. Read them, and what we say for a Church-Covenant, 't may save charge and time in reading other Bookes; remember wee strive not here for masteryes, but give an account of our practise, wherein if thou know'st we faile Candidus imperti; if we agree let us worke by our plat-forme; and may thy soule flourish as a greene heath or watered garden. So prayeth

Thine heartily

H. PETER.

THE XXXII
QUESTIONS
STATED.

1. **W**Hether the greatest part of the English there (by estimation) be not as yet unadmitted to any Congregation among you, and the Reasons thereof?

    2. what things doe you hold to be Essentiall and absolutely necessary to the being of a true Visible Church of Christ?

    3. whether doe you not hold all Visible Believers to bee within the Visible Church as Members thereof, and not without in the Apostles sence, 1 Cor. 5. and therefore ought so to be acknowledged, and accepted in all Congregations wheresoever they shall come, and are so knowne: and ought (if they desire, and be not otherwise unfit') of right to be permitted to partake in all Gods ordinances and Church priviledges there, so farre as they personally concerne themselves, although they be not as yet fixed Members in particular Covenant, either with that Congregation where for the present they reside, nor with any other?

    4. whether you doe not hold that Baptisme rightly (for

sub-

substance) *partaked doth make them that are so Baptized, Members of the Visible Church: and so to have right (at least quoad nos) to all the priviledges thereof (so farre as they are otherwise fit) untill they be cast out (if they so deserve) by Excommunication.*

5. *Whether doe you not admit Children under age as Members of the Church, together with, and in the Admission of their Parent or Parents: So as thenceforth they may partake of all Church priviledges (being otherwise fit) without any other personall profession of Faith, or entring into Church Covenant, when they shall come to yeares? and how long doe you count them under age?*

6. *Whether do not you admit Orphants under age, with and in their Guardians?*

7. *Whether doe you admit or refuse Children under age only accoding to the present estate of their nearest Parents? Or doe you not admit them if any of their next Ancestors before their parents were believers?*

8. *Whether doe you require of all persons of age, whom you admit Members of any Church?*

    1. *A publike vocall declaration of the manner and soundnesse of their conversion?*

    2. *A publike profession of their faith concerning the Articles of Religion.*

    3. *An expresse verball covenanting to walke with the said Church in particular, in Church fellonship.*

    4. *And not to depart from the said Church afterward without the consent thereof: or how doe you hold and practise in these things?*

9. *Whether doe you hold all, or the most of our Parish assemblies in Old-England to be true Visible Churches of Christ; with which you may lawfully joyne in every part of Gods true worship (if occasion served thereto:) or if not all or the most,*

then

*then what ones are those of which you so account, and with which
you durst so partake or joyne; and in what respects? And why
be not the rest such as well as they?*

10. *If you hold that any of our parishionall Assemblies are
true Visible Churches, and that the Members thereof are all,
or some of them (at least) members of true visible Churches,
then whether will you permit such members (at least) as are either famously knowne to your selves to be godly, or doe bring
sufficient Testimoniall thereof from others that are so knowne,
or from the Congregation it selfe whereof they were members
here, to partake with you in all the same Ordinances, and
parts of Gods true worship in any of your Congregations (as
by occasion they may be there) in the same manner, and with the
like liberty, as you would permit any that might happily come
unto you from any of the Churches of* Geneva, France, *the*
Low-Countreyes, *or yet from any one Church to another a-
mong your selves: Suppose from some Church about* Connecticut, *or that of* Plimouth, &c. *Vnto the Church at*
Boston, New-Towne, Dorchester, &c. *Or if not, what
may be the Reason thereof?*

11. *Whether doe you hold our present standing in our Parish Assemblies here in* Old ENGLAND, *to bee lawfull and
safe to be continued in, or how farre it may be so?*

12. *Whether doe you hold that every Believer is alwayes
bound to joyne himselfe as a fixed Member to some one particular Congregation, so as if he doe not, and so oft and so long
as he doth it not, so oft and so long he is without the Church in
the Apostles sence,* 1 Cor. 5. *as an Heathen or Publican, out
of the Kingdome of Christ, and possibility of salvation, according to that maxime in divinity,* Extra Ecclesiam non
est salus.

13. *Whether doe you thinke it lawfull and convenient
that a company of private and illitterate persons (into a Church
body combined) should themselves ordinarily examine, elect,*

ordaine,

ordaine, and depose their owne Ministers of the word, without the asistance of any other Ministers of other Churches, where the same may be had?

14. Whether doe you hold that every small Company of seaven, or nine, or twenty, or fourty persons, combined into a Church body, be such a Church (as by the ordinance of Christ) hath, and ought to have all power, and exercise of Church Government: So as they may transact all Ecclesiasticall businesses independently amongst themselves?

15. Whether do you give the exercise of all Church power of Government to the whole Church, or to the Presbiters thereof alone? and if to those, then we desire to know what act of Government, and Superior authority (properly so called) may the Presbiters doe, more then any other member may doe, or without the particular consent of the rest, wee crave to have those particular Acts mentioned: and how, and over whom in those Acts the Presbiters doe rule (in propriety of speaking) more then the rest of the Congregation doe?

16. Whether doe you not permit Women to Vote in Church matters?

17. Whether in Voting doe the Major part alwayes, or at any time, carry Eccl-siasticall matters with you, or in what things doth it, in what not?

18. What meanes have you to preserve your Churches in Unity and Verity, or to correct or reduce any Church erring in Doctrine or practice.   As,

1. Whether you have any plat-form of Doctrine and Discipline agreed upon: or if you have not, whether meane you to have one, and when; and thinke you it lawfull and expedient so to have?

2. Whether have you combined your selves together into Classes, or purpose so to doe, so as to doe no weighty matter without their counsell and consent?

3. Or

3. *Or give you any power to Synods and Councells to determine and order things that cannot otherwise be ended, so as that their determination shall bind the particular Churches so assembled to due obedience, in case they decree nothing but according to Truth and right, and to peaceable suffering, in case they should doe otherwise? Or what other course you have, or intend to have for that end aforesaid?*

19. *Whether hold you, that each particular Church may lawfully make such Laws or Orders Ecclesiasticall, for the Government of it selfe, and the Members thereof; for decency, order, and Edification, as shall oblige all her Members, and may not be omitted without sinne?*

20. *Wherein hold you that the whole Essence of a Ministers calling doth consist: As 1. whether is Election by the People it, yea or no? Or 2. is it so Essentiall, as that without it, the Ministers calling is a meere nullity? Or 3. is Ordination as Essentiall a part thereof, as the Peoples Election? Or 4. is it but a meer formality and solemnity of their calling?*

21. *Whether doe you hold it lawfull for meer lay or private men to ordaine Ministers in any case?*

22. *What Essentiall difference put you between the Office of Pastor and Teacher, and doe you observe the same difference inviolably; and do not your Teachers by vertue of that Office give themselves usually to application of doctrine as, well as your Pastours? and do they not also usually apply the Seales?*

23. *What authority or Eminency have your Preaching Elders, above your sole Ruling Elders, or are they both equalls?*

24. *Whether may a Minister of one congregation (being thereto requested) do as a Minister any act of his Ministery (as Preach, Baptize, Administer the Lords Supper, Ordain, &c. in and unto other Congregations besides his owne?*

25. *Whether hold you that a Minister of a Congregation,*

leaving,

leaving or loosing his place (suppose without his fault) doe withall lose both Nomen *and* Esse *of his ministery, and do become a meere Lay, or private man, untill he be a new elected, and ordained?*

26. *Whether doe you allow, or thinke it lawfull to allow and settle any certain & stinted maintenance upon your Ministers?*

27. *Whether doe you permit and call upon meer Lay and private men (neither being in the ministerie nor intended to it) ordinarily to preach or Prophecie publiquely, in, and before the Congregation? and whether thinke you that prophecying mentioned, 1* Cor. 14. *be to be understood of such, and be an ordinary and standing order of God in the Church?*

28. *Whether doe you allow and call upon your people publiquely before all the Congregation to propound Questions, move doubts, & argue with their ministers of matters delivered either by them or others, either at the same, or some other time?*

29. *Whether hold you that the conversion of sinners to God is ordinarily the proper fruit and effect of the word Preached, by a* Minister *alone, and that by vertue of his Office alone, or that it is alike comman to ministers, and Lay persons, so they be gifted to preach?*

30. *Whether all and every of your Churches (including* Plimouth, &c. *) do precisely observe the same course both in Constitution and Government of themselves?*

31. *Whether would you permit any Companie of Ministers and People (being otherwise in some measure approvable) to sit downe by you, and set up and practise another forme of Discipline, enioying like libertie with your selves in the Commonwealth, and accepted as a sister Church by the rest of your Churches?*

32. *Whether hold you it lawfull to use any set forms of Prayer in publique or private, as the Lords prayer and others, either made by himselfe that useth the same, or else by some other man?*

THE

THE
ANSWERS
TO THE
Aforegoing QUESTIONS.

The first Question Answered.

LL the English and others also are freely admitted to be present in our Congregations, at the reading of the Scriptures, and exposition thereof (which is wont alwayes to goe along therewith) at the preaching of the word, singing of Psalmes, Prayers, Admitting of Members, and dispencing of Censures; And many also are admitted to Church Communion, and so to partake in Church Ordinances and priviledges, as Sacraments, power of Election, Censures, &c. hough many also there are who are not yet admitted to the Church Communion. But whether is the greater number, those that are admitted hereunto, or those that are not we cannot certainly tell? But in the Churches in the Bay, where most of us are best acquainted, we may truely say, that for the heads of Families, those that are admitted are farre more in number then the other: besides whom there are likewise sundry children.

dren and Servants that are Admitted alſo. And for the Reaſons why many are not yet received to Church Communion, they are ſundry. 1. Many are not admitted becauſe
they are not yet knowne. Every yeare hitherto God hath
repleniſhed the Country with many new commers, and
theſe at the firſt are not ſuddainly taken in, as Members of
Churches, till by time there have been ſome triall of them,
and better occaſion to know them what they are. Sometimes once a yeare there are in the Land many hundreds,
and ſome thouſands of this ſort. 2. When by time they
come to be knowne many do appeare to be carnall, and give
no Teſtimony of being Members of Chriſt, and therefore
if they ſhould offer themſelves to be Members of Churches
the Churches would not ſee Warrant to receive them, becauſe the Church is the body of Chriſt. 3. Some that are
Godly do of their own accord for a time forbeare to offer
themſelves, till they be better acquainted with the Church
and Miniſtry where they intend to joyne, and with the
wayes in which the Churches walke in this Country, and
and till they be better informed what are the duties of
Church Members. 4. Thoſe that are knowne to be Godly, are all admitted in ſome Church or other preſently, upon their own deſire, when they offer themſelves thereto :
except any have given offence by walking (in any particular in their Converſation)otherwiſe then becomes the Goſpell; and then ſuch are to give ſatisfaction to them to whom
they have given offence, by acknowledgeing their offence,
and ſhewing repentance for it,and then they are Admitted.

To. 2.   It is one thing what Churches ought to be by the appointment of Jeſus Chriſt, another, what weakneſſe and
ſwervings from his appointment, he may beare withall for
a time, before he renounce and caſt off a People from being
his Church. In reſpect of the former our Anſwer is, That
when a Viſible Church is to be errected, planted or conſtituted, by the Appointment of Chriſt, it is neceſſary that
the matter of it, in regard of quality, ſhould be Saints by
calling,

calling, Visible Christians and Believers, 1 *Cor.* 1.2.*Eph.*1.1. And in respect of Quantity no more in number in the dayes of the New Testament, but so many as may meet in one Congregation. 1 *Cor.*11.20 & 14.23.*Acts* 14.27.& 15.22 30. And the forme, a gathering together of these visible Christians,a combining and uniting of them into one body, by the bond of an holy Covenant, for which we refer you to the Apolgie of the Churches in *N. E.* sent the last yeare in way of Answer to Mr. *Bernard.* For the latter we deny not, but visible Churches rightly constituted at the first, may degenerate, and great corruptions may grow therein, both in respect of matter and forme, and likewise in respect of their walking and Administrations, and yet the Lord in his patience may beare long with them,before he give them a Bill of Divorce, and make them *Lo-ammi*, not a People ; as the example of the Church of Israel in the old Testament. Of the Church of *Corinth*, the Churches of *Galatia*, the 7 Churches of *Asia*, and others in the New Testament, doe abundantly manifest. But what degrees of corruption may be, before the soule as it were, and life, and being of a Church be destroyed, is hard for us precisely and punctually to determine ; or to say thus farre a Church may erre, and yet remaine a Church ; but if it proceed any further, then it ceaseth to be a Church any more ; onely in the generall this we observe, the Lord doth not presently cast off a Church or give them a Bill of Divorce, no not for fundamentall errors in Doctrine, or Idolatry in Worship, or Tyranny in Government, till after obstinate and rebellious rejection of Reformation, and the meanes thereof : for all these were found in the Church of *Israel* when they crucified Christ, yet the Apostles rejected them not, till after the light of *Grace* offered, and blasphemously rejected, *Acts* 13. 45. 46. But if your selves have so Studied this point, as to have ripened and formed thoughts therein, we should gladly receive light from you.

We do not know any visible Church of the *N. T.* pro- To: 3.
B   perly

perly ſo called, but onely a particular Congregation ; and therefore when this Queſtion in the firſt and laſt clauſe of it ſpeakes of Believers within the viſible Church as Members thereof, although they be not Members of that particular Congregation, where for the preſent they reſide, nor of any other : this ſpeech ſeemes to us according to our apprehenſion to imply a contradiction. They that are within the viſible Church as Members thereof, muſt needs be Members of ſome particular Congregation, becauſe all viſible Churches are Congregationall, as Mr. *Baine* ſheweth at large from the Church of *Antioch, Act.* 14. 27. the Church at *Corinth,* 1 *Cor.* 11. & 14. and other examples and Reaſons with Anſwers to the objections to the contrary in his *Dioceſ. Triall Queſt.* 1. Whereto we referre you in this Point ; neither is he alone in this Tenent, for Mr. *Parker,* and many other teach the ſame. Thoſe ſilenced and deprived Miniſters that wrote the Booke called, *The Chriſtian and modeſt offer of Diſputation*, laying downe 16. Propoſitions which they offer to maintaine againſt the Prelats, give this for the fourth of them *viz. There is no true viſible Church of Chriſt, but a particular ordinary Congregation onely.*

Doubtleſſe every true viſible Church hath power from Chriſt to exerciſe Excommunication and other Ordinances of Chriſt, ſo that they proceed therein according to the Rules of the word, 1 *Cor.* 5. 4. 5. *Mat.* 18. 17. Now Dr. *Whitakers* ſheweth againſt *Bellarmine,* that Excommunication belongs not to the univerſall Church, but onely to a particular Congregation. *Qui juſtè excommunicantur,* ſaith he, *eo ſacana trajectos eſſe concedimus, non tamen poſſe propriem, Dici ejectos ex Eccleſia Catholica, Quia Excommunicatio non Catholica, ſed particularis Eccleſia cenſura eſt* De Eccleſ. Qu. 1. c. 6. Wherefore if Excommunication which belongs to the viſible Church, belongeth to a particular Congregation, it followeth, that there is no viſible Church, but onely a particular Congregation. Secondly, As all viſible Believers are not without Chriſt, but in Chriſt, according as they are believers, ſo we eaſily grant, that thoſe without, of whom the

Apoſtle

Apostle speakes, 1 *Cor.5.* were unbelievers, Pagans, and Heathens, both without Christ, and also without the visible Church. For those that were in Christ, and believers in Him, were not wont to abstaine from joyning to some particular Congregation or other; and so it come to passe, that as they were in Christ by their Faith, so by such joyning they became also to be within the visible Church. 3. But this we conceive is cleare also, that unlesse Believers, be Members of this or that particular Congregation to whose inspection and Government they have commended themselves in the Lord, they also in some respect may be said to be without, that is without the jurisdiction and power of the visible Church, and without right to the priviledges of it, as long as they continue in that State: for the Church hath nothing to do, either to dispence censures and Church priviledges to Pagans, who are without all Churches, and without *Christ* also; or to such Christians, who though they are not without *Christ*, yet are not within any particular Church: for neither the Church, nor the Ministers thereof may be ἄλλοτ ιοϊπίσκοϊοι. And though those without of whom the Apostle speakes, 1 *Cor.* 5. were Pagans and Heathens, both without *Christ*, and without the visible Church also, yet when hee speaketh of Judgeing, and saith they might judge them that are within, and not judge them that are without, hee must not be understood as if he meant it simply of being in Christ or without Christ, and no more then so, but also of being in that particular Congregation, and without it: for it is plaine, that those that were in *Christ*, if they were not also within their particular Congregation, they had nothing to do to judge them; and those that were within their particular Congregation, them they might judge, though they were not in *Christ*. 4. And that Church priviledges do not belong to Believers, as such, but onely to such as withall are Members of some particular Church: the Grounds and Reasons in the Answer to the third and fourth Proposition sent the last yeare, do seeme to us to make manifest, whereto we do referre you, for further Answer to this Question. B 2 It

To : 4.   It is an opinion of the Anabaptiſts, that the Church is made by Baptiſme, and therefore when they conſtitute or erect a Church, they do it by being all of them Baptized, which was the manner of Mr. *Smith,* Mr. *Helxis,* and the reſt of that company when they ſet up their Church : The Papiſts alſo do imagine, that men enter into the Church by Baptiſme, and it is ſaid, that their Founts were ſet neere the doores of their Temples, to ſignifie mens entring into the Church by Baptiſme, and they thought themſelves to be chriſtened, or made chriſtian ſoules by being Baptized. But we do not believe that Baptiſme doth make men Members of the Church, nor that it is to be Adminiſtred to them that are without the Church, as the way and meanes to bring them in, but to them that are within the Church, as a ſeale to confirme the Covenant of God unto them. For

1. This is one point of the dignity and priviledge of the Church, that Baptiſme and all Church Ordinances are given and committed to it, as Circumciſion, and Church Ordinances were given and concredited to the Church of the Jewes, *Ioh.* 7. 22. Now if Baptiſme in its firſt being and inſtitution be given as a benefit and priviledge to the Church, then Baptiſme is not that which makes the Church; but the Church is preſuppoſed, and muſt be before it, for the dones, or perſons to whom a thing is given, muſt needs be before the gift that is given to them.

2. The nature and uſe of Baptiſme is to be a ſeale to confirme the Covenant of Grace between God and his Church, and the Members thereof, as circumciſion alſo was, *Rom.*4.11. Now a ſeale is not to make a thing that was not, but to confirme ſomething that was before ; and ſo Baptiſme is not that which gives being to the Church, nor to the Covenant, but is for confirmation thereof. To bring in Baptiſme before the Covenant, and before the Church, with whom God makes the Covenant and then to bring in the Church afterwards, is to make Baptiſme a ſeale unto a Blanke, or to a falſhood. When the Jeſuits of *Rhemes* had ſaid that *Chriſt*

                                                              ſent.

sent 12 Apostles to the Jewes to move them to penance, and so by Baptisme to make them of his Church. And that *Paul* was sent to the Gentiles to move them also to faith and penance, and by Baptisme to make them of his Church. This saying of making men of the Church by Baptisme, though uttered by them, as it were by the way, and not being the chiefe scope of their discourse, yet seemed to Mr. *Cartwright* so erroneous and unsound, that hee would not let it passe without bearing speciall witnesse against the same. And therefore in opposition thereunto he hath these words, and in another Character for more conspicuousnesse, *viz.* That Baptisme makes not men of the Church, but sealeth their incorporation into it, hath been declared afore. *Argument* of *Acts* 6. 1. And that Catechisme which is commonly said to be penned by our Reverend Brother Mr. *Ball*, or Mr. *Nicholas*, now with God, giving this for the definition of Baptisme, that it is a Sacrament of our ingrafting into Christ, communion with him, and entrance into the Church, doth in the Exposition plainely declare, that when they called Baptisme a Sacrament of our entrance into the Church, they did not meane that Baptisme made men Members of the Church, but signified and sealed that they were Members afore : The seed of Abraham say they, *Pag* 144. *Gal.* 3. 7. or children of Christian Parents are within the Covenant, are Christians and Members of the Church, 1 *Cor.* 7. 14. *Rom.* 11. 16. Baptisme therefore doth not make them Christian soules, but doth solemnly signifie and Seale their ingrafting into Christ, and that communion which the Members of *Christ* have with him their head, and doth confirme, that they are acknowledged Members of the Church, and entred into it, 1 *Pet.* 3. 21.

3. The Lord hath had his Church when there was neither Baptisme nor circumcision, and therefore Baptisme or circumcision cannot be that which constitutes the Church. The Church is one and the same in essence from the beginning of the world to the end thereof, *viz.* A company of People combined together by holy Covenant with God,

and

and one with another, and this hath been before Baptifme
and likewife betore Circumcifion in the dayes of the Patri-
arks afore *Abraham.* Yea it Baptifme now, or Circumcifion in former time did make men Members of the Church,
then for forty yeares together there was no making
Members of the Church, for fo long circumcifion was
difcontinued, when Baptifme was not yet inftituted,
Iofſ.5.2, 3.&c. And fo by this meanes all that Generation of
the Ifraelites that were not circumcifed till their comming
over *Jordan* unto *Gilgall* fhould have bin no Members of the
Church afore that time of their circumcifion, which is contrary to the Scripture, which as it gives the name and title of
a Church to the body of this people, when they were in the
Wildernefſe, *Act. 7. 38.* (and they were in the Wildernefſe
40. yeares, in the latter parts of which time there were few
left remaining that had beene circumcifed) fo it witneſſeth
that afore this time of their circumcifion they were in
covenant with God and his Church, *Deut. 29. 10, 11, 12.*
For that covenant was not made with their Fathers that
came out of Egypt, and were circumcifed there, becaufe that
generation was confumed in the Wildernefſe for their mur-
muring afore this time : but this covenant was made with
the children, that as yet were uncircumcifed, and therefore
it was not circumcifion that made men Members of the
Church.

4. Baptifme hath been Adminiſtred, and no Church nor
Membersmade thereby and men have been made Members
of Churches and not then Baptifed, but before. And ther-
fore it is not Baptifme that makes men Members of the
Church. Jerufalem and all Judea, and all the Region round
about Jordan were Baptifed of *Iohn* confeſſing their finnes,
Mat. 3. 6. And Chriſt made and Baptifed more Difciples
then *Iohn*, *Ioh. 4. 1.* And yet neither Chriſt nor John did
make new Churches, nor gather men into them themfelves,
both the one and the other living and dying Members of
the Jewifh Church, which was not yet diſſolved, untill upon their rejecting of Chriſt (not onely of his perfon upon
the

the croffe, but of his Gofpel in blafpheming and perfecut-
ing Grace offered them) the two ftaves of beauty and bands
were broken and cut affunder, whereby God did breake the
Covenant that he had made with that People, and the Brotherhood between Juda and Ifrael, that is, he did un church
them, *Zach.* 11. 10, 11. &c. to 15. So that here is Baptifme Adminiftred by John and Chrift, and yet men not
received thereby into the Church as Members, for they
were Members long afore.

Againe, when any of thofe of Jerufalem, Judea, and the
Region round about Jordan, that were Baptifed of John, or
any of thofe, many more that were Baptifed of Chrift,
were afterward joyned as Members to thofe chriftian
Churches in Judea, Samaria, and Galile, *Act.* 9. 31. (As
no doubt many of them were) they were not made Members of thofe Chriftian Churches by being Baptifed, for
they were Baptifed long afore by John and Chrift, fo that
thofe men were Members of the Jewifh Church, which
was not yet diffolved, and were Baptifed afterward. And
therefore it was not Baptifme that made them members,
either of the one Church or of the other.

5. There are fundry inconveniences, which for ought we
fee will unavoidably follow, if we fhall fay that Baptifme
makes men members of the Church; For firft, if Baptifme
be that which conftituts the Church, then Baptifme may
be difpenced by them that are no Minifters, for extraordinary Minifters, as Apoftles, and fuch like are now ceafed; and
ordinary Minifters have no power to difpence Baptifme to
any, but onely to them that are already members of the
Church, feeing their Commiffion and power is limited to
the Church, and the flock of God over which the Holy
Ghoft hath made them overfeers, *Acts* 20. 28. Befides, the
Church is before the Minifters, feeing the power of choo-
fing Minifters is given by Chrift unto the Church; and ther-
fore if Baptifme be that which makes the Church, then
men muft be Baptifed afore there be Minifters to Baptife
them, and confequently without Minifters.

Secondly,

Secondly, if Baptifme rightly for fubftance partaked, doth make men members of the vifible Church, then it will follow that Papifts are members of the Church: for they have Baptifme fo farre right for fubftance, as that it needs not be repeated. But Mr. *Perkins* teacheth that this Baptifme proves not the Church of *Rome*, of which all Papifts are members, to be any true Church of God, and gives fundry Reafons for the fame, in Anfwer to them, that from Baptifme rightly for fubftance Adminiftred in Popifh Affemblies, would prove thofe Affemblies to be true Churches : *Expofit. of Creede*, in the Article, *I believe the holy Catholique Church.*

And furely for our parts we doe not fee how it will be avoyded, but if Baptifme made men members of the vifible Church, either Papifts are members of the vifible Church, and the Church of *Rome*, of which they are Members, a true vifible Church, or elfe we muft renounce their Baptifme as corrupt and falfe, even for the fubftance of it; and fo all fuch as fhall be converted from amongft them, muft be Baptifed againe, as not having had the fubftance of Baptifme before : fuch dangerous confequences do follow from faying, that Baptifme, rightly for fubftance partaked, doth make them that are fo Baptifed Members of the vifible Church.

Object.   If any fhall fay, *Though Baptifme do not make men Members of the Church, yet it proves them to be Members as a caufe, is proved by the effect, or an Antecedent by a confequent : and therefore all Baptifed Perfons fhould be admitted to all Church priviledges as Members, where ever they become.*

Anfw.   We Anfwer, that this will not hold neither, but fuppofe a man have received Baptifme as a Member of fome vifible Church, which ought not to have been Adminiftred to him, had he not been a member, yet this doth not prove him to be a member ftill and fo give him right to all Church Priviledges, though hee do remaine alwaies as a Baptifed perfon ; and the Reafon is, becaufe his Baptifme may remain, when his Church fellowfhip may be diffolved, as that he can have no right to Sacraments thereby : the
Church

Church member-ship of a Baptifed Perfon may be thus diffolved by fundry meanes. 1. By fome fentence of Excommunication juftly paffed againft him for his finne ; for
that cenfure puts him away from the Communion of the
Church, 1 *Cor.* 5. 2 13. and makes him as an Heathen or
Publican, *Mat.* 18. 17. So that in that cafe he can have
no right to Sacraments by his Member-fhip, though he ftill
continue a Baptifed Perfon. 2. By his voluntary departing from the Church and the communion of the fame
when it is unjuftly done, 1 *Ioh.* 2. 19. *Iude* 19. *Heb.* 10. 25.
In which cafe Dr. *Ames* refolves fuch Schifmaticks to be no
Members of the vifible Church, *Caf. Conf. Lib.* 5 *c.* 12 *Q* 4.
Refp. 3. 3. By the diffolution of the Church of which he
was a Member ; for Church Member-fhip is in relation to
a Church, and therefore if the Church ceafe, the Member-
fhip muft ceafe alfo ; *Relatum & correlatum Qua talia funt fi-
mul, adeoque fe mutuo ponunt et tollunt.* Now a Church may
be diffolved, 1. By Apoftacie and Gods giving hem a bill
of Divorce thereupon. *Ier.* 3. 8. When yet there may be in
fuch a Church fome particular perfon or perfons deare to
God, who in fuch a cafe are bid to come out from fuch
an Apoftate Church. *Rev.* 18 4. *Hofe.* 2. 1, 2. & 4, 15, 17.
2. By death, as by fome grievous Peftilence or Maffacre, &c.
in which cafe one particular perfon furviving, cannot be
counted a Member of a Church, when that Church is ex-
tinct of which he was, and yet he remaines a perfon Baptifed if he were Baptifed afore. 3. If that be true which is
taught by Dr. *Ames caf. Conf. Lib.* 5. *c.* 12. *Q.* 3. *Refp.* 2. that
in fome cafes it is lawfull and neceffary to withdraw from
the communion of a true Church (which feemes to be
agreeable to grounds of Scripture, *Ephef.* 5. 11. 2 *hro.* 11 14)
then that will be another cafe wherein Church Member-
fhip is difanulled ; for how a man can be counted in that
ftate a Member of a Church, when hee hath lawfully and
neceffarily withdrawn himfelfe from the communion of
the Church, we do not underftand. And this fhall fuffice
for Anfwer unto this Point, whether Baptifme make men

C   Members

Members of a visible Church, which as we conceive, is the scope and drift of this Question. Yet before we proceed to make Answer to the next, something also may be said concerning some passages in your Amplification of this fourth Question. As first concerning those words wherein you aske, *Whether they that are Baptised have not right,* quoad nos, *to all the priviledges of the visible Church* (so farre as they are otherwise fit:) concerning which words we may say,

1. That those words of your Parenthesis *(so farre as they are otherwise fit:)* doe plainely imply, that in your judgement, though one hath received Baptisme, yet this doth not give him right to the priviledges of the visible Church, unlesse other things do concurre to make him fit, wherein we consent with you. Now if this be so, then this seemes to be an Answer to that which (as we conceive) is the maine intent of the Question. For how can it be, that Baptisme alone should give men right to the priviledges of the Church (as Members thereof, as the Question seemes to import) when in the Amplification of it, it is granted, that Persons Baptised have no such right, except other things doe concurre to make them fit: we doe not see how these things doe stand together.

Secondly, those words *as farre as they are otherwise fit:)* as they seeme to imply that which contradicts the maine scope of the Question ; so they are so generall and of such a latitude, as that when the Question is Answered, the Reader is still left at uncertainty : For if such a Parenthesis may be annexed *(so farre as men are otherwise fit:)* then the like Question may be applied to many other things besides Baptisme, and would receive the very same Answer, as in case of Baptisme it would receive. As for example, if one should aske whether Morall honestie or litterall knowledge in the Scriptures, or Historicall Faith, or the use of Reason, whether any of these doe not give men right to Church priviledges, so farre as they are otherwise fit ? You know the Answer would be, Yea. For though none of these be sufficient alone, to give men right to the priviledges of the
                                                                Church,

Church, yet they are such as they that have them, have right so farre as they are otherwise fit, and so if it were granted that they that have received Baptisme have right, as you say, to all the priviledges of the Church, so farre as they are otherwise fit : yet as this doth not prove that Baptisme alone doth give men such a right, so still it remaines to be considered, and more particularly declared, what those other things are that besides Baptisme must concurre to make one fit; and unlesse those things be expressed in particular, the Question with such a generall Qualification as is here set down, may be Answered affirmatively, and yet the Reader will be still in the darke, and as much to seeke as before.

Lastly, those words in the latter end of this Question had need to be further cleared, wherein you aske, *Whether Baptised persons have not right to all the priviledges of the Church,* quoad nos, *antill they be cast out by Excommunication?* For suppose an open Blasphemer, a Sabath-breaker, an Adulterer, a Drunkard, *&c.* that deserves to be Excommunicated, be not proceeded against according to rule, but be suffered to continue in the Church through bribery or other corruption of the times, would you say that such a person had right either before God, or *quoad nos* to all the priviledges of the Church, onely because hee is Baptised? Surely your words doe import so much, unlesse that Parenthesis *(so far as they are otherwise fit)* may be any helpe in this case. And yet we hope you doubt not but such Doggs and Swine have no right either *quoad nos,* or otherwise, to the priviledges of the Church as long as they continue in that State, although they have received Baptisme, and although through the sinfull neglect of men they be not cast out by Excommunication, as they doe deserve; For if grosse sinners have such right to Church priviledges, onely because they are Baptised, then by what right can the Church cast them out by Excommunication, as you seeme to confesse that she may : for can she cast men out from such priviledges whereunto they have right? doubtlesse such proceedings were not

C 2   right,

right, unleſſe the Church have ſuch a Tranſcendent power as the Apoſtles never had for they could do nothing againſt the truth but for the truth, nor had they any power for deſtruction, but for Edification, 2 *Cor.* 13. 8. 10. Wherefore we dare not ſay ſuch men have right to Church priviledges (*quoad nos*) untill they be actually caſt out, becauſe before they be caſt out, it muſt be cleare to the Church, that they have no ſuch right, or elſe ſhe can have no lawfull Right to caſt them out.

To 5. & 6.   1. Infants with us are Admitted Members in and with their Parents, ſo as to be Admitted to all Church priviledges of which Infants are capable, as namely to Baptiſme; and therefore when Parents are once Admitted, their Children are thereupon Baptiſed, if they were not Baptiſed afore, as ſometimes it falls out. 2. But whether they ſhould thereupon be admitted to all other priviledges when they come to age, without any perſonall profeſsion of Faith, or entring into Church Covenant, is another Queſtion, of which by Reaſon of the Infancy of theſe Churches, we have had no occaſion yet to determine what to judge or practiſe one way or other. 3. But for the preſent this we would ſay; It ſeemes by thoſe words of your Parentheſis (*being otherwiſe fit*) you do acknowledge, that Children of Church Members are not to be admitted to Church priviledges, unleſſe they be fit, wherein we conſent with you as counting it altogether unſafe, that Idiots, Franticks, or perſons openly ungracious and prophane, ſhould be admitted to the Lords Table, though they were the Children of Church Members, and thence we may inferre the neceſsity of their perſonall profeſsion of their faith, when they come to yeares, and taking hold of Church-Covenant, whereby we meane onely a Renewing of Covenant, or a new profeſsing of their Intereſt in Gods Covenant, and walking according to it, when they ſhall be *Adulti*: for otherwiſe we do confeſſe, Children that are borne when their Parents are Church Members, are in Covenant with God even from their birth,

birth, *Gen.*17.7.12. and their Baptiſme did ſeale it to them.
But notwithſtanding their Birthright, we conceive there is
a neceſſity of their perſonall profeſſion of Faith and taking
hold of Church-Covenant when they come to yeares
(though you ſeeme to thinke it not needfull:) for without
this it cannot ſo well be diſcerned ; what fitneſſe is in them
for the Lords Table and other Church priviledges, as by
this meanes it might? And inaſmuch as entring into
Church-Covenant is nothing elſe but a ſolemne promiſe to
the Lord, before him and the Church, to walke in all ſuch
wayes as the Goſpel requireth of Church Members, if they
ſhall refuſe to make any ſuch promiſe, and ſhall be unable,
or unwilling to make any profeſſion of their Faith, when it
is required of them, this would be an evidence againſt them,
of their unfitneſſe for Church priviledges, inaſmuch as they
openly breake that Rule, 1 *Pet.* 3. 15. Be ready to give a
Reaſon of the hope that is in you with meekneſſe and feare.
What hope is there that they will examine themſelves when
they eat of that Bread and drinke of that Cup, 1 *Cor.* 11. 28.
Who when others do examine them they are unable or unwilling to give Anſwer? Or how ſhall we thinke that they
will receive the Lords Supper worthily, or walke as becomes
the Goſpel if they do refuſe to profeſſe or promiſe any ſuch
matter? Wherefore in this Point we cannot but fully approve the practiſe of the Reformed Churches, among whom
it is the manner as *Zepperus* writeth, to admit Children that
were Baptiſed in their Infancy unto the Lords Table, by
publique profeſſion of their Faith, and entring into Covenant, *conſuetum eſt,* ſaith he *ut qui per ætatem, in que Doctrina
Catechetic a profectum ad ſacram Cœnam primum admittuntur, fidei
confeſſionem coram tota Eccleſiâ publicè edant,* &c. *Polit. Ecleſ. l.*
1. *c.* 14. *p.* 158. that is, The manner is, that they who
by reaſon of age and proficiency in the Doctrine of Cate-
chiſme are firſt Admitted to the Lords Supper, ſhould publiquely before the whole Church, make confeſſion of their
Faith, being brought forth into the ſight of the Church by
their Parents, or them that are inſtead of Parents, at the

appoint-

appointment of the Minister : and likewise should promise
and Covenant by the Grace of God to continue in that faith
which they have confessed, and to leade their lives according to it : yea and moreover, to subject themselves freely
and willingly to the Discipline of the Church ; these words
we see are full and plaine, that Children are not in those
Churches received to the Lords Table without personall
confession of Faith, and entring into Covenant before.

4. But how long Children should be counted under age,
and whether Orphans are not to be admitted with their
Guardians (which is your sixt Quæry) we should be willing
to heare your judgement therein, as having of our selves
hitherto had no occasion to search into those Questions ;
onely this we thinke, that one certaine rule cannot be given
for all, whereby to determine how long they are under age,
but according as God gives experience and maturity of naturall understanding, and Spirituall ; which he gives sooner to some then unto others.

To 7.   Such Children whose Father and Mother were neither
of them Believers, and sanctified, are counted by the Apostle (as it seemes to us) not fæderally holy, but uncleane,
what ever their other Anceftors have been, 1 *Cor.*7.14. And
therefore we Baptise them not.   If you can give us a sufficient Answer, to take us off from that Scripture, 1 *Cor.* 7.
which seemes to limit this fæderall sanctity or holynesse to
the Children whose next Parents one or both were Believers, we should gladly hearken to you therein ; but for the
present, as we believe we speake, and practise according to
our light.   And if we should goe one degree beyond the
next Parents, we see not but we may goe two, and if two,
why not 3, 4, 20, 100, or 1000 ? For where will you stop ?
And if we shall admit all Children to Baptisme whose Anceftors within a thousand Generations have been Believers,
as some would have us, we might by this Reason Baptise
the Children of *Turkes,* and of all the *Indians,* and *Barbarians*
in the Country ; for there is none of them but they have
                                                         had

had some Believing Ancestors within lesse then a 1000. Generations, it being farre from so much since *Noah* and his Sonnes came out of the Arke.

We do believe that all Members of Churches ought to be *To 8.* Saints, and faithfull in Christ Jesus, *Eph.* 1. 1. 1 *Cor.* 1. 2. *Col.* 1. 2. *Phil.* 1. 1. and thereupon we count it our duty to use all lawfull and convenient meanes, whereby God may helpe us to discerne, whether those that offer themselves for Church Members, be persons so qualified or no: and therefore first we heare them speake concerning the Gift and Grace of Justifying Faith in their soules, and the manner of Gods dealing with them in working it in their hearts; which seemes to be your first particular in this Quæry. Secondly, we heare them speake what they do believe concerning the Doctrine of Faith, so taking a tryall what measure they have of the good knowledge of the Lord, as knowing that without knowledge men cannot well Examine themselves and discerne the Lords body, as Church Members ought to doe when they come to the Lords Table. And hereby also we would prevent (as the Lord shall helpe us) the creeping in of any into the Church that may be infected with corrupt opinions of Arminianisme, or Familisme, *&c.* or any other dangerous error against that faith which was once delivered to the Saints, as knowing how easily such men if they were admitted, might infect others, and perhaps destroy the Faith of some. And this seemes to be intended in your second particular. For both these we have our warrant as in Generall, from those places which shew how Church Members ought to be qualified, that they ought to be Saints, faithfull in Christ Jesus, *&c.* So in speciall from that, *Math.* 3. 6. *Acts* 19. 18. & *Acts* 8. 37. 38. Where men before they were admitted, made profession of Repentance towards God, and faith towards the Lord Jesus Christ; for it is expressely said, that they confessed their sinnes, they confessed and shewed their deeds, they professed their faith in Jesus Christ the Sonne of

of God. Thirdly, when this is done, thoſe that by mani-
teſtation of Repentance and Faith are approved ; as fit
Members for a Church do openly profeſſe their ſubjection
to the Goſpel of Chriſt, and to all the Ordinances of God
in that Church, where now they joyne as Members, which
ſeemes to be your third particular in this Quærie. The Diſtinction of particular Churches one from another, as ſeve-
rall and diſtinct Societies, ſeemes to us a neceſſary ground
for this practiſe ; for without this kinde of Covenanting,
we know not how it would be avoyded, but all Churches
would be confounded into one, inaſmuch as it is neither
Faith, nor inure affection, nor Towne-dwelling, nor fre-
quenting the Aſſemblies that can make a man a Member,
or diſtinguiſh Church Members from other men: See the
Apologie.

4. Your fourth particular in this Quærie is Anſwered in
the Anſwer to the ſixt Poſition ſent the laſt yeare : Beſides
all theſe, we heare the teſtimony of others, if there be any
that can ſpeake of the converſion and Godly converſation
of ſuch perſons : which we judge to be a warrantable courſe
from *Acts* 9. 26, 27.

To 9.   It is the ſecond of your Quæries, what things we held neceſſary to the Being of a true viſible Church in Generall :
which being Anſwered ; this of the Pariſh Aſſemblies in
England in particular, whether we hold all or the moſt of
them to be Churches, we conceive might well have been
ſpared. They that know the ſtate of thoſe Aſſemblies may
make application of the Generall to the particulars, if they
have a calling therunto. Yet becauſe you are pleaſed to put
us to this alſo, we thus Anſwer. 1. That we doubt not but
of Ancient time there have been many true Churches in
England conſiſting of right matter, and compacted and united together by the right forme of an holy Covenant. For
Mr. *Fox* ſheweth at large, that the Goſpel was brought into
England in the Apoſtles times, or within a little while after,
Acts & Mon. lib. 2. begining *p.* 137. Where hee reporteth
out of *Gildas*, that *England* received the Goſpel in the time
of

of *Tiberius* the Emperor, under whom Christ suffered; and that *Joseph* of *Arimathea* was sent of *Philip* the Apostle from *France* to *England*, about the yeare of Christ 63. and remain-ed in *England* all his time, and so hee with his fellowes laid the first foundation of Christian Faith among the Brittaine people, and other Preachers and Teachers comming after-wards, confirmed the same and increased it. Also the said Mr. *Fox* reporteth out of *Tertullian*, that the Gospel was disperced abroad by the sound of the Apostles into many Nations, and amongst the rest into Brittaine, yea into the wildest places of Brittaine, which the Romans could never attaine unto, and alledgeth also out of *Necephorus*, that *Simon Zelotes* did spread the Gospell to the West Ocean, and brought the same into the Iles of *Brittanie*, and sundry other proofs he there hath for the same Point. Now if the Gospel and Christian Religion were brought into *England* in the Apostles times, and by their meanes, it is like there were Churches planted there of Saints by calling (which is the right matter of Churches) and by way of holy Covenant, as the right form : for that was the manner of Constituting Churches in the Apostles times, as also in the times afore Christ, as hath been shewed from the Scripture in the Apo-logie. And the footsteps hereof (though mixed with mani-fold corruptions that have growne in aftertimes) are re-maining in many places of the Land to this day, as appea-reth by those 3 Questions and Answers at Baptisme. *Abre-nuntias? Abrenuncio; Credis? Credo: Spondes? Spondeo: Dost thou renounce the Devill and all his works? I renounce them all. dost thou believe in God the Father, &c? I do believe. Dost thou pro-mise to walk according to this Faith &c? I do promise.* For though it may be they conceived, that men entred into the Church by Baptisme, yet hereby it appears that their judgment was that, when men entred into the *Church* there ought to be a renouncing of sin, and believing on *Christ*, and an open pro-fessing of these things, with a promise to walk accordingly.

Secondly, Though Popish Apostacy did afterwards for many ages over spread all the Churches in *England* (as in other Countries) yet we believe God still reserved a rem-nant according to the Election of Grace amongst them, for

whose

whose fake he reserved the Holy Scriptures amongst them, and Baptisme in the name of the Trinity onely. And when God of his rich Grace was pleased to stirre up the Spirit of King *Edward* the sixth, and Queene *Elizabeth* to cast off the Pope, and all fundamentall errors in Doctrine and Worship, and a great part of the Tyranny of Popish Church Government, though at first some Shires and sundry Parishes stood out against that Reformation for a time, yet afterwards they generally received the Articles of Religion agreed upon *Anno* 1562. which are published and consented to by all the Ministers endowed in every Congregation, with the silent consent also of the people, and subscription of the hands of the chiefe of them ; wherein they do acknowledge no rule of Faith or manners, but the holy Scriptures; no divine Worship but to God onely; no mediation nor salvation but in Christ onely : no conversion by mans free will, but by Gods free Grace : no Justification but by Faith : no perfection nor merit of works, with sundry other necessary and saving truths ; all which containing the Marrow and Summe of the Oracles of God (wich are the λόγια, the *eloquia Dei,* concredited onely to the Church. *Rom.* 3. 1. 2. and which are that saving Doctrine of truth, which is fruitfull in all the world where it comes, *Colo.* 1. 5, 6. and upon which the Church is grounded and built, and which also it holdeth forth and maintaineth, 1 *Tim.* 3. 15.) we do therefore acknowledge, that where the people do with common and mutuall consent, gather into setled Congregations ordinarily every Lords day, as in *England* they do, to heare and teach this Doctrine, and do professe their subjection therunto, and do binde themselves and their Children (as in Baptisme they do) to continue therein, that such Congregations are true Churches, notwithstanding sundry defects and dangerous corruptions found in them, wherein we follow the judgement of *Calvin Instit.* 4. 1. 9. 10. &c. *Whitakers de notis Ecclesia cap.* 17. and many other Divines of chiefe note : nor can we judge or speake harshly of the Wombes that bare us, nor of the paps which gave us suck.

Thirdly, But inasmuch as grievous corruptions of latter yeares have greatly increased in some of those Assemblies

(as

(as we heare) both in Doctrine, in Worship, and in the Go-vernment thereof, besides those that were when some of u-were there, and in former Yeares : Therefore we are not with-out feare (and with griefe we speake it) what things may com unto at length. If Corruptions should still increase and grow, they might come in time(if the Lord be not more mercifull)ur-to such an height as unto obstinacy in evill, and to wilfull re-jection of Reformation, and the meanes thereof; and then you know it might be just with God to cast off such utterly, out of the account and number of his Churches ; so as never to walke among them any more : which we heartily pray the Father of mercies to prevent that such a day may never be: But if *Ephe-sus* repent not of her declinings, the Lord hath threatned that *he will come unto her quickly, and remove her Candlesticke*; that is, he will un-Church them, *Rev.* 2. 4,5. and *Lukewarme Laodi-cea shall be spewed out of his Mouth, Rev.* 3. 16. And therefore it behoves such of them to Repent, and Reform themselves betime, lest the Lord deale with them as he hath done with others.

And it much concernes your selves (in hearty love and faith-fullnesse we speake i·, and so we desire you wou'd accept of it) it very much concernes you (deare Brethren) whil'st you live amongst them, to beare faithfull witnesse against the corrupti-ons that are remaining in any of them, in respect of their Con-stitution, Worship, Discipline and Ministerie, lest by any sinne-full silence or slacknesse of yours that should blow the Trumpet and stand in the gap, the breach should be made wider, and the iniquity increase;and lest men should flatter themselves in their sinnes, under the Name and Title of the true Church, as the Jewes thought themselves secure because of the Temple of the Lord, *Jer.* 7. 4.

4. Because you would know not onelie whether we count those Assemblies to be Churches, but what wee would doe for joining in Gods Worship in them, if occasion served thereun-to : We Answer, that if we were in *England*, we should wil-lingly joine in some parts of Gods true Worship, and namely in hearing the Word, where it is truely Preached in sundry Assemblies there ; Yea though we doe not know them to bee Churches, or knew not what they were, whether true Churches or no ? For some Worship, as Praier, and Preaching,and Hea-

D 2   ring

ring the Word, is not peculiar to Church Aſſemblies, but may
be performed in other meetings. *Mars-hill* at *Athens* was no
Church, nor the Priſon at *Philippi*, and yet the Word of GOD
was Preached and heard lawfully with good ſucceſſe in theſe
places, *Act.* 17. and *Act.* 16. How much more might it bee
lawfull to heare the word in many Pariſh aſſemblies in *England*,
in which generally there is a profeſſing of Chriſt; and in many
of them: Many Soules that are ſincere and upright hearted
Chriſtians, as any are this day upon the face of the Earth; and
many Congregations indeed that are the true Churches of Jeſus Chriſt, *See* Mr. *Robinſons* Treatiſe of the lawfullneſſe of
hearing the Miniſters in the Church of ENGLAND.

5. But why we durſt not partake in their preſcript Lyturgie,
and ſuch Ordinances though true, as are adminiſtred therein;
We gave you account the laſt Yeare, in Anſwer to the firſt and
ſecond Poſition: As alſo in an Anſwer to a Diſcourſe of that
Subject, Penned by our Reverend Brother Mr. *Ball*. What we
have done in our ignorance whilſt we lived amongſt you, wee
have ſeene cauſe rather to bewaile it in our ſelves here, then to
it in others there.

To 10. Our Anſwer to this Queſtion is this, 1. That we never yet
knew any to come from *England* in ſuch a manner as you do here
deſcribe (if the things you mention may be taken *conjunctim*, and
not ſeverally) *viz*: to be Men famouſly known to be godly, and
to bring ſufficient Teſtimoniall thereof from others that are ſo
knowne, and from the Congregation it ſelfe, whereof they were
Members: We ſay we never yet knew any to come to us from
thence in ſuch a manner, but one or other of the things here mentioned are wanting: and generally this is wanting in all of them,
that they bring no Teſtimoniall from the Congregation it ſelfe:
And therefore no marvell if they have not beene admitted (further then before hath been expreſſed in Anſwer to Queſt. 1.) to
Church Ordinances with us, before they have joyned to one or
other of our Churches; for though ſome that come over bee
famouſly knowne to our ſelves to be Godly, or bring ſufficient Teſtimoniall with them from private Chriſtians, yet neither
is our knowledge of them, nor Teſtimonal from private Chriſtians ſufficient to give us Church-power over them, which wee
had

had need to have, if we muſt diſpence the Ordinances of Church communion to them? though it be ſufficient to procure all due Reverent reſpect, and hearty love to them in the Lord.

2. If the things mentioned were all to be found, yet it would be alſo requiſite (if they would partake of Church Ordinances with us, and yet not joyne to any of our Churches) that woe ſhould know the Congregation it ſelfe, from which they come, not onely to be a true Church, but alſo what manner of one it is: For ſuch perſons cannot communicate with us in Church Ordinances in their owne right; becauſe they joine not as Members in any of our Churches; but it muſt be in right of the Congregation in *England*, to which they doe belong, and by virtue of the communion of Churches, and ſo our admitting of them to communion with us in ſuch a manner, and upon ſuch termes, is not only an Act of Communion with the perſons themſelves, but alſo with the Congregation of which they are: Now as we cannot of Faith admit men to Church Ordinances, which we believe belong only to Church Members; unles we know the Congregation of which they are Members to be a true Church. So ſomtimes a Congregation may be ſo corrupt, that though it doe remain a true Church, yet for the corruption and impurities of it, it may be lawfull and neceſſary to withdraw communion from the ſame (for which Dr. *Ames* gives ſundry grounds and Reaſons, *Caſ. Couſ. lib. c.* 12. *Q.* 3. *Reſp.* 2.) or at leaſt to proteſt againſt ſome groſſe corruptions therein. In regard whereof we had need to have ſome knowledge and information what that Congregation is, with whom now we have Church communion; when in their right wee admit men into communion, that wee may know how to admit ſuch Men, and what to require from them more or leſſe. And this together with that want of teſtimoniall from the congregation is one maine Reaſon, why ſome few godly men that have come from *England* upon occaſion, not with purpoſe of continuance here, but of returning againe; have not beene received to Church Ordinances during their abode in the Countrey (though this we may ſay alſo, that we know not of any ſuch that have requeſted to be received) whereas ſuch as have come in like manner from one Church to another amongſt our ſelves, upon their requeſt have been received: the Reaſon we ſay is, becauſe theſe Churches are better

　　　knowne

knowne then the Parish Assemblies are.

3. But if men come from one Church in this Countrey to a-
nother with purpose there to stay, and not to returne to the
Church from whence they came, (which is the manner of all,
or the most that come from *England*) they are not received into our Churches; but upon the very same tearmes, and in the
same manner, as men are received that come from *England*; viz:
upon personall profession of their faith, and entring into Church
Covenant, in that Church to which they now come (And the
same we say of such as come from any of the Churches in other
Countries) and wherefore are they not received otherwise, because we renounce the Church of which they were Members
as no true Church? Not so, but because wee believe in matter
of Faith, (such as is the admitting of Members) any true Church
may erre: and there may now bee seene some unworthinesse in
the man which did not appeare when hee was admitted in the
other Church: and therefore no reason that the Act of one
Church in the admitting of Members or the like, should bee a
binding Rule unto another; for all Churches are left to their
liberty to admit and receive such into their Church; as they shal
find to be fit according to the Rule of the word, and to refuse
others, without respect of what they have bin before, whether
Members of this Church, or that Church, or of any Church, or
none: and therefore in this, our walking and practice, is alike towards one another, and towards others as it is towards yours.
In which practise we are not alone, for the very same as Mr. *Parker* reporteth, is the manner of the Reformed Churches, a-
mongst whom, no man is admitted for a Member; but upon
personall profession of faith, and entring into Church covenant,
though it may be he have formally beene admitted in the very
same manner in the Church where he lived before, *Polit. Eccles.
l. 3. c. 16. 3, 4. p. 171.*

To 11.

If the ground of this Qu. were any doubt in your owne consciences concerning your owne way, there were no fault in propounding such a Qu. for further light and satisfaction, if wee
were able to give it. Or if it did arise from any unnecessary in-
termedling of ours in your matters, so as to take on us to condemne or judge your present standing, when we have no calling

ling thereunto, there were then Reason why we should give account of our owne doings or sayings. But if it came from some men we should looke at it as a tempting Question, tending onely to make matter, and pick quarrells; and then we should leave it to them that framed it, to confider the ground of it; and to frame their owne Anfwer to it. As for us, we have alwayes been flow and loth to judge or condemne your prefent ftanding; remembring the faying of the Apoftle, *Who art thou that judgeft another Mans Servant, he ftandeth or falleth to his own Mafter,* *Rom.* 14. 4. But now knowing you well (Reverend and Deare Brethren) and your integrity, we thinke wee may lawfully and fafely Anfwer, and that wee would doe by premifing a few diftinctions, for explaining the Termes of the Queftion.

1. Concerning the perfons in the Parifh Affemblies, which may be meant of fuch as the providence of *God* hath fo difpof'd that they are free and at liberty: or of fuch as are bound, and it may be not *fui juris,* as Wives, Children under the government of Parents, Servants, Apprentices, Prifoners, Sicke-folkes, &c.

2. Concerning the Parifh Affemblies, which may bee meant either of fuch as want the Preaching of the Word or Sacraments, or Difcipline, or any other holy Ordinance of Chrift, or have many Ordinances in them which are not of God, but of Men: or elfe it may be meant of fome others, which in both refpects are R formed and pure, if there be any fuch.

2. Concerning ftanding in them, which may be meant onely of habitation, and dwelling upon Houfe or Land within the Precincts of the Parifh; or elfe in conformirg in judgement or practife to the corrupt Eccefiafticall Ordinances ufed in thofe Affemblies; and contenting themfelves therewith.

4. Concerning lawfull and fafe; where fafety may be meant either of fafety from finne, or from danger by perfecution, thefe Diftinctions wee judge neceffary to bee premifed, becaufe your Queftion is, whether wee count your ftanding in the Parifh Affemblies lawfull and fafe; or how farre it may be fo? And fo our Anfwer is in 3. Propofitions.

1. Some Perfons, and namely thofe that are not *fui juris,* may lawfully and without finne; though it may bee not fafely without danger of perfecution, continue fuch ftanding in the Parifh

Affemb-

Assemblies, as doe dwell within the Præcincts of them, so long as they neither conforme themselves to the corruptions of men by such continuing of their standing, nor live in the neglect or want of any Ordinance of CHRIST through their owne default.

2. Such standing in the Parish Assemblies, where a man shall, and must conforme to the corruptions of men, in Doctrine or Worship; or the Government of the Church, is not lawfull for any to be continued in.

3. To continue such standing in the Parish Assemblies, as to live in the want of any Ordinance of Christ is not lawfull, nor can be done safely without sinne of them, to whom the providence of God doth open a doore of further enlargement.

The first of these Propositions wee suppose you doubt not of.

The second is confirmed by many places of Scripture; and namely by such as these. *Though Israel play the Harlot, yet let not Iudah offend, and come not yee to Gilgall, nor go up to Bethaven, nor sweare the Lord liveth: Ephraim is joyned to Idolls, let him alone,* Hos, 4. 15 17. *Come out from among them, and be ye separate saith the Lord, and touch no uncleane thing, and I will receive you,* 2 Cor. 6. 17. *Be not partaker of other Mens sinnes, keep thy selfe pure,* I Tim. 5. 22. *Come out of her my People, that yee bee not partakers of her sinnes, and that yee receive not of her Plagues,* Rev. 18. 4. *Have no fellowship with the unfruitfull works of darkenesse, but reprove them rather,* Eph. 5. 11. *Ephraim is oppressed and broken in judgment; because he willingly walked after the Commandement,* Hos. 5. 11. *Wee ought to obey God rather then Men,* Act. 4 19. and 5. 29. *Jeroboam* made Priests of the lowest of the People, which were not of the sonnes of Levi, and ordained a Feast in the fifteenth day of the Eight Moneth, in the Month which he had devised of his owne heart, &c. and then the *Levites* left their Suburbs and their possessions, and came to *Iudah* and *Ierusalem,* for *Ieroboam,* and his Sonnes had cast them off from executing the Priests Office unto the Lord; and after them out of all the Tribes of Israell, such as set their hearts to seek the Lord God of Israel, came to *Ierusalem* to Sacrifice to the *Lord God* of their Fathers, I *King.* 12. 31, 32, 33. with 2 *Chron.* 11. 14. 16. Vpon these and such like grounds of holy Scripture

ture we are perſwaded that ſuch ſtanding in the Pariſh Aſſemblies, as this ſecond Propoſition mentions, is not lawfull for any to be continued in. And we hope, you doubt not of the truth of this ſecond Propoſition neither, though we are afraid that many Chriſtians, when it comes to practice, doe ſinfully pollute themſelves by partaking in the Ceremonies, and other corruptions in the prayers, in the Doctrine, and in the Miniſtery remaining in ſundry of thoſe Aſſemblies, whom it will bee your part wh.lſt you live among them faithfully and by all good meanes to inſtruct and teach, and exhort, to ſave themſelves from the corruptions and pollutions of the times and places wherin they live; as well in this particular of Church matters, and Gods Worſhip as in other things: Wherein wee wiſh with all our hearts that our ſelves when time was, had been more watchfull and faithfull to God and the ſoules of his People, then the beſt of us were: The Lord lay not our Ignorance to our charge.

The third Propoſition may bee made good ſundry wayes, 1. By precepts, wherin we are commanded to obſerve all things whatſoever Chriſt hath commanded, *Mat.* 28. 20. to ſeeke the Kingdom of God and his Righteouſneſſe, *Mat.* 6. 33. to yeild our ſelves unto the Lord, and to enter into his Sanctuary, 2 *Chr.* 30. 8. And therefore we may not pleaſe our ſelves to live in the neglect of any Ordinance which he hath inſtituted and appointed. 2. By examples, for the Spouſe of Chriſt will not reſt ſeeking her beloved untill ſhee finde him in the fulleſt manner, *Cant.* 1. 7, 8. and 3. 1, 2. &c. and the ſame minde was in *David*; as appeares by his heavy Lamentation, when he wanted the full fruition of Gods Ordinances, and his longings, and prayer to be reſtored thereto, *Pſal.* 63. and *Pſal.* 42. and 84. although he enjoyed *Abiathar* the High Prieſt, and the Ephod with him; and likewiſe *Gad* the Prophet, 1 *Sam.* 23. 6, 9, 10. &c. 1 *Sam.* 22. 5. when good *Ezra* in his journey from *Babilon* to *Ieruſalem*, viewing the People at the River *Ahava* found none of the Sonnes of *Levi* there, afore he would goe any further, he ſent unto *Iddo* a the place *Caſiphia* for Miniſters for the Houſe of God, *Ezra* 8. 15. 16. &c. And when being come to *Ieruſalem* they found by the law, that it was an Ordinance of God to dwell in Boothes, and keepe the Feaſt of Tabernacles in the ſe-

E   venth

venth Month, they preſently ſet upon the practice thereof, in the
appointed ſeaſon; when the like had not beene done in Iſrael,
from the dayes of *Ioſhua* the ſon of *Nun* unto that day, *Neb.* 8.
14. &c. Yea, and our Lord Jeſus himſelfe, though hee had no
need of Sacraments, to be to him any ſeale of Remiſſion or for-
giveneſſe of ſinnes, yet in conſcience to the Ordinance of GOD,
(that he might fullfill all righteouſneſſe, *Mat.* 3. 15.) and for
our example, did both obſerve the Paſſover, and likewiſe was
Baptized, and did eat with his Diſciples at his laſt Supper. All
which examples being written for our learning, doe ſhew us
how farre wee ſhould bee from contenting our ſelves to live in
the Voluntary want of any Ordinance and appointment of
G O D.

3. There is none of the Ordinances of Chriſt, but they are
needfull and very profitable in the right uſe of them to the ſoules
of his Servants: And therefore they ſhould not be neglected.
To thinke of any of them, as things that may well bee ſpared;
and therefore to content our ſelves to be without them, is to call
in queſtion the wiſdome of him that did appoint them, and to
make our ſelves wiſer then God.

4. Our owne infirmities and Spirituall wants are ſuch, as
that wee have continuall need of all the holy meanes which the
Lord hath appointed, for ſupplying what is wanting in us; for
correcting what is amiſſe; and for our continuance and growth
in grace. Hee is a proud man, and knowes not his own heart
in any meaſure, who thinkes he may well be without any ſpirituall Inſtitution and Ordinance of Jeſus Chriſt. Upon theſe and
ſuch like ground, we hold it not lawfull nor ſafe, for any Chriſtian that is free, to continue ſuch ſtanding in the Pariſh Aſſemblies where he cannot enjoy all the ſpirituall and holy Ordinances of Chriſt. And hereupon we do exhort you lovingly in the
Lord, to take heed that this be not the ſinne of any of you, nor
of any other, whom your example may embolden thereunto:
For neceſſity is laid upon you, and upon all Chriſtians, by theſe
and ſuch like grounds of the holy word of the Lord; That neither yor, nor others doe live in the voluntary want of any holy
Ordinance of Chriſt Jeſus, but either ſet them up, and obſerve
them in the places where you are; or elſe (if you bee free) to
remove for the enjoyment of them, to ſome place where they
may

may be had; and it may be of the two, rather this latter. For sometimes if Israel Sacrifice to their God in the Land, they shall Sacrifice the abomination of the *Egyptians* to the Lord : And lo say they, *shall wee sacrifice the abomination of the Egyptians before their eyes, and will they not stone us?* It is better therefore in such a case to goe into the Wildernesse, and to do it there, *Exo.* 8. 25. 26, 27. *Hos.* 2. 14. *Mat.* 10. 23.

Obj: *As for that opinion that may be in the minds of some, that if any Ordinance of God be wanting, it is the sinne of them that are in Authority, and they must answer for it? But the people of God may without sinne, live in the want of such Ordinances as Superiors provide not for them.*

Answ: The Answer hereunto is, that indeed the Ordinances of God may more peaceably and quietly bee observed where the Commandement and countenance of Magistrates is afforded; for then is fulfilled the saying that is written, *Kings shall bee thy nursing Fathers, and Queens thy nursing Mothers,* Esa. 49. 23. and doubtlesse it is a great blessing, when God (that hath the hearts of Kings and Princes in his hands, *Prov.* 21. 1.) doth incline them to favour, and further the service of the House of GOD, as somtimes he doth, even when themselves are Alients and Strangers. *Cyrus, Darius,* and *Artaxerxes,* gave great countenance and incouragement to the Jewes to build the House of God, *that they might offer sacrifices of sweet savour to the God of Heaven, and pray for the life of the King and of his Sonnes,* Ezra 6. 8, 9, 10. In which case good *Ezra* blesseth the Lord, that had put such a thing into the Kings heart, to beautifie the House of the God of Heaven, *Ezra* 7. 27. And therefore *Kings and all in Authority, should be prayed for, that we may lead a godly and peaceable life, in Godlinesse and honesty,* 1 Tim. 2. 1, 2. Neverthelesse, the things that are ordained and commanded of GOD, the observing of them in a peaceable way (yeilding due reverence to all that are in Authority, and praying for them) this observing of the Ordinances of God cannot be unlawfull, for lack of the Commandement of Man, as appeares by the doctrine and practice of the Apostles, *Act.* 4. 19. & 5. 29. and the approved practise of Believers in their times, if they had neglected the Ordinances of God, and namely Church Ordinances, till they had had the commandement of Magistrates therein, such neglect would have

E 2

beene their grievous finne, and for ought we know they might have lived and died without them, the Magistrates at that time being all either Heathens or Jewes, yet enemies; and if Church Communion and the exercise of such Ordinances, as Christ hath appointed for his Churches, was lawfull, and needfull, and profitable, when Magistrates were enemies to the Gospell; and bee not fo when Magistrates doe professe the Gospell, we doe not fee but Christians may fometimes be lofers by having Christian Magistrates, and in worfe condition, then if they had none but profeffed Enemies. Befides this, if Superiors should neglect to provide bodily fuftenance for them that are under their charge; we doe not thinke that any Mans Confcience would be fo fcrupulous, but hee would thinke it lawfull by all good meanes to provide for himfelf in fuch cafe, rather then to fit fill and fay, if I perifh for hunger, it is the finne of them that have Authority over mee, and they muft anfwer for It: Neither can we tell how the Confcience of any Christian can excufe himfelf, if he thinks not the Ordinances of Christ, as neceffary for the good of his foule, as food is neceffary for his temporall life; or doe not willingly in this fpirituall hunger break through ftone Walls as the Proverbe is, and runne from Sea to Sea to feeke God in his owne way, rather then to perifh without fpirituall food, becaufe others provide not for him.

And this is our Anfwer to this eleventh Quere, concerning your ftanding in the Parifh Affemblies: which Anfwer of ours, and the exhortation therein, as we pray the Father of mercies to make effectuall by his bleffing for thofe good ends, which wee intend therein, fo wee cannot in the fame, but reflect upon our felves and our owne wayes in times paft; as feeing not a little caufe to judge our felves before the Lord, as long as wee live, for our finfull ignorance and negligence, when wee were in *England*, o obferve and walke according to thofe Rules of the Word, which now upon occafion given by this Qu. wee doe commend to your felves and other Chriftians. The Lord in mercy pardon our offences, and direct your felves and his fervants in our deare Native Countrey, both in remaining and removing to doe that which is pleafing in his fight.

To 12.   Whereas this Qu. in the firft claufe and laft but one compared
together

together speakes of Believers out of the Kingdome of GOD, and possibility of salvation, we conceive it is a contradiction, for those that are true Believers, cannot be out of possibility of salvaion, but possibly may, yea most undoubtedly shall bee saved, *Joh.* 3. 16. and 5. 24. the contrary whereof is to overthrow all the promises of the Gospell, and with the Papists and Arminians to establish falling from grace.

2. For that saying, *Extra Ecclesiam non est salus*, wee conceive it cannot be universally true, if it be meant of the visible Church, which in the New-Testament is a particular Congregation; but onely being taken for the Church invisible, or the Vniversall Church, which is the whole company of the elect in Heaven, in Earth, and not yet borne, *Ioh.* 10. 16. and 17. 20. out of which elected Company there is not one that shall be saved, nor any of the elect neither, but in the way of Regeneration, *Ioh.* 3. 3. but as for the Visible, we believe the old saying is true, *there are many Wolves within, and many Sheepe without*, Joh. 10. 16. and therefore it cannot be universally true, that out of the Visible Church there is no salvation: Inasmuch as all Chrifts Sheepe shall be saved, *Ioh.* 10. 28. of whom yet notwithstanding there are some not joyned to the Visible Church: If the Thiefe that repented on the Crosse was a Gentile, as it was possible he was; then hee was uncircumcised, and then it will trouble a Man to tell of what Visible Church he was: and yet there is no doubt but he was saved. The like may be said of *Iob* and of his friends, of whose salvation we make no question, and yet it is a great question whether they were of any Visible Church or no, inasmuch as the Visible Church in those times seemed to be appropriated to the House and posterity of *Abraham, Isaac,* and *Iacob,* of which line & race it cannot easily be proved that all these men did come, nor that they joined themselves in Visible fellowship with that Church. The Centurion, *Mat.* 8. 10. and the Woman of *Canaan, Mat.* 15. were both of them believers and saved, and yet it doth not appeare that they were members of the Visible Church of the Iews, which was the only visible Church of God in those times.

Men of yeares ought to be believers, and so in the state of Salvation afore they be joyned to the Visible Church, and therefore there may be salvation out of that Church: For it is possible

that

that such an one as being a Believer is fit to bee joyned to the Church may die and depart this life afore hee can bee joyned, as that good Emperour *Valentinian* 2. died before hee could bee baptized. And for your selves if you should thinke that Baptisme makes men members of the Visible Church;as is intimated in your fourth Question: you may not then deny but there may be salvation out of the visible Church: unlesse you will say that there is no salvation without Baptisme,which we believe is farre from you to imagine.

3. We doe hold that so oft and so long as a believer doth not joyne himselfe as a Member to some particular Congregation or other,so oft and so long he is without the Church in the Aposties sence, 1 *Cor.* 5. for the Church in the Aposties sence, is a particular Congregation;for he writeth to,and of the Church at *Corinth*, which Church was a particular Congregation, 1 *Cor.*5,4,& 14.23.& 11.17.20,and having power of judgeing her own Members (as all visible Churches have) yet had no power of Judgeing any,but such as were within that particular Congregation, as all them they had power to judge, whether they were believers in Christ or no. Mr. *Baine* (as we said before) is very large and cleare in proving this Position, that the Churches instituted by Christ and the Apostles, were only such as might meet in one Congregation ordinarily , and answers many objections to the contrary,*Dioces.tryal.Q.1.*

4. For the Question it selfe, we hold that every believer (if possibly he can) is alwayes bound to joyne himselfe as a Member to some particular Congregation or other; and yet not because,else he is a Heathen and Publican, or out of possibilitie of salvation,as this Question suggests,but upon other grounds.

1. Because of the Commandment of God, *Cant.* 1.8. *Math.* 6.10.33.

2. Because willingly not to doe this is a secret disparagement to the wisdome of God that hath ordained Churches with giving power and privilegdes therunto,*Mat.*18.17. 1 *Cor.*5.4. and promises of his gracious presence to be with them amongst them, *Mat.*18.20. *Rev.* 2.1. *Exod.* 20.24. Now to what end were all these, if believers should live and not joyne themselves to some Church? These priviledges and promises would in such case be all in vain,and the mercy of God offered therin,unthankfully neglected.

3. Volun-

Thirdly, voluntarily abstaining from joyning to the Church is noted and condemned as a sinne, *Heb.* 10.25. and a signe of fearefull unbelievers, *Act.* 5.13. of the rest durst no man joyne unto them.

Fourthly, good men in Scripture have been forward in practise this way, *Isay* 2.2,3. *Zach.* 8.23. *Act.* 2.41,42. and 9.26. and have mourned with much bitternesse when they have been deprived of Liberty so to doe, *Isay* 56.3. and *Ps.* 42. and 63. and 84.

Fiftly, this joyning is a part of that Order, and orderly walking which is required of believers, *Col.* 2.5. *1 Cor.* 14.40.

Sixtly, If Believers doe neglect this joyning, it is not onely a wrong to themselves, but also a great unkindnesse to God: for if one believer may doe this, why not another, and if two why not three, foure &c. and if all believers should doe thus, God should have no visible Churches upon Earth, unles he will acknowledge the Assemblies to be of *unbelievers* Churches: for as stones in the *Mountains* are not an house untill they be joyned together, though they be digged up out of the Quarry, and squared & hewn, and hereby are made fit to be joyned together, and so to become an house : so believers are not a Church till they be joyned in holy Covenant in some Congregation, though the worke of Grace and Faith in their soules have made them fit, and meete to be a Church of God, which is the House of the living God : or as the humane soule and body are not a man unlesse they be united; so Christian or believers are not a visible Church without visible union into some particular Congregation. Mr. *Perkins* having said that forth of the militant Church : there are no meanes of salvation, no preaching of Gods word, no invocation of Gods Name, no Sacraments, and therefore no Salvation ; concludes with these words ; For this cause every man must be admonished evermore to joyn himselfe to some particular Church, being a sound Member of the Catholick Church, *Expos.* of *Creed* in the Article of the Church; and Doctor Ames gives 6. Reasons, why every Christian should joyne himselfe to some particular Church or other *Cas.Confc.* L. 4. c. 24. Q. 1. and in another place he hath these words. *Illi igitur qui occasionem habent*

habent adjungendi ſeſe Eccleſiæ, & eam negligunt, graviſsimè pec-
cant, non tantum in Deum ratione Inſtitutionis, ſed etiam in ſuas
proprias animas ratione benedictionis adjuncta, etſi obſtinatè perſi-
ſtant in ipſa incuria, quicquid alias profitentur, vix poſſunt haberi
pro fidelibus Regnum Dei verè quærentibus. Medul. Theol. *l.*
1. c. 32. Sect. 28.

To 13.   Firſt, whereas this 13th. Queſtion ſpeakes of private
and illiterate perſons into a Church Body combined, wee
looke at this as an incongruous expreſſion, if not a contradiction. For a company ſo combined as to make a Church,
are not fitly called private, (though they be illiterate in reſpect of humane learning) in as much as a Church or a
Church-body, eſpecially in times and places of peace and
liberty, is a publike Congregation and ſociety : and the acts
of Communion which they have among themſelves (ſuch
as is the election and depoſing of Miniſters, whereof the
Queſtion makes mention) are not private acts, but publike
or people-like. Neither are literate or learned men therefore publike, becauſe they are indued with humane learning, unleſſe withall they be called to publike office or im-
ployment in Church or Common-wealth : and therefore if
illiterate be an *exegeſis* of private, we conceive that *exegeſis* is
not good.
     Secondly, whereas this Queſtion asketh *Whether it be lawfull*
and convenient that ſuch a company ſhould themſelvs ordinarily exa-
mine elect, ordain and depoſe their owne Miniſters? if *ordinarily* be
as much as *frequently*, we anſwer three things. Firſt, that if
one Church doe frequently come to ſuch actions, that is, to
take in and put out the ſame men, this is not without ſuſpi-
tion of much levity and raſhneſſe in the people, or unfaith-
fulneſſe or unworthy walking in the Miniſters, or both ;
and therefore *ordinarly*, that is, *frequent* taking in and putting out againe in this manner, is as much as may be to be
avoided. Secondly, when ſuch things doe often and frequently fall out, it is doubtleſſe a Judgement of God upon
ſuch a people to have ſo many changes in their Miniſters ;
as was that of which it was ſaid, *three ſhepheards have I cut off*
in one moneth, *Zach.*11.8. that People ſhould be ſo oft as
                                                              ſheep

sheep having no Shepheard ; *for the transgression of a land many are the Princes thereof, Pro.28.2.* So in like sort for the transgressions of a Church many are the Ministers thereof ; we meane,when they have many Ministers,by the comming in and going out of the same men, or the removing of some and the taking in of others in their roome : for otherwise, it is a blessing of God, when a Church is furnished with variety of Ministers at the same time, *Acts* 13.1. & 21.18. *Phil.*1.1. Thirdly, yet this word (*ordinarily*) doth seeme to imply, that in your judgement sometimes this may be lawfull and convenient to be done ; Now upon the same ground on which it may be done sometimes,upon the same it may be done at other times, if there be just occasion.

Thirdly, for the assistance of the Ministers of other Churches, of which this Question maketh mention › if this be onely by way of counsell or advice, we know nothing unlawfull or inconvenient in such assistance, because Churches are as Sisters one to another, *Cant.* 8.8. And therefore it is our practice in ordination of Ministers,as also in removall of them, to have such assistance. But for authority and power, we know none that Ministers have properly so called in any Congregation or Church, save that one,over which the Holy Ghost hath made them overseers : and therefore we thinke it not lawfull nor convenient, when a Church is to ordaine Officers, to call in such assistance (*viz.* by way of authority or power) of the Ministers of other Churches.

Fourthly, we judge it lawfull and convenient that every Church of Christ (what ever their humane learning be, whether much or lesse) should elect and choose their Ministers : God doth not (for ought we know) give this power of calling their owne Ministers unto such Churches as have many learned men in them, and deny it unto others ; but gives it indifferently to every Church,as they are a Church, and so to one Church as much as to another If we thought you doubted whether the power of calling Ministers were given by Christ unto the Church, we might here alledge many Reasons for it ; but this being the constant judge-

F   ment

ment of the eminent Lights of this age, and the former who have been studious of Reformation, wee must hope (till we hear to the contrary) that your selves do not differ from them in this point. As for us, those grounds and reasons from the holy Scripture which are alledged by 1 *Calvin,* 2 *Zanchius,* 3 Mr *Cartwright,* 4 Dr *Ames,* and (5) others doe satisfie us in this particular. (1) *Institut* 4.3.14. 15. (2) *De redemp. in* 4.*præcep.p.*1015.1016. &c. who alledgeth *Bucer* and *Musculus.* (3) 1.*Reply p.*44.*&c.* (4) *Medul. Theol.l.*1.*c.*21.*Sect.*30 *& caf.confc.lib.*4.*c.*25. *Q.*5. (5) *Demonist.of disc.c.*4.

Fifthly, as for that objection which seemes to be implyed in the word *illiterate,* that it should not be lawfull or convenient for a body to choose their owne Ministers because they are illiterate or want men of humane learning among them, wee further answere thereto; first, that among us when a company are to be combined into a Church-body, (as you speake) there is usually one or other among them who doe not want all humane learning but have been trained up in Universities, and usually have been Ministers and Preachers of the Word in our native Countrey and approved by the godly there; and are here by the company that doe so combine intended to be chosen afterwards for Pastors or Teachers: and accordingly, after the Church is gathered, are in due time elected and ordained into their places. Secondly, but yet if there were none such among them at their first combining and uniting, we doe not see how this could hinder them of liberty to choose Ministers to themselves afterward, when God shall send any to them that may be fit for the worke; because this is a liberty that Christ hath purchased for them by his precious bloud and they that are fit matter to bee combined into a Church-body, are not so illiterate but they have learned the Doctrine of the holy Scripture in the fundamentall points thereof; they have learned to know the Lord and their owne hearts, they have learned Christ, the need they have of him, and of all the meanes of enjoying him, the worth that is in him, and the happinesse laid up for them in him: and

therefore

thereforethey may not be reproached as illiterate or un-worthy to choose their owne Ministers: nay, they have the best learning, without which all other learning is but mad-nesse and folly, and science falsly so called, 1 *Tim.*6.20. and indeed of none account with God, nor available for dire-ction and guidance in the affaires of the house of God, such as is this election of Ministers, nor for the salvation of the soule in another world, 1 *Cor.*1.19 20. & 2.14. *Job* 32.8.9. though it may be, and is very usefull therewith. Thirdly, you know, and (we doubt not) doe abhorre as much as wee the spirit of those men that are proud of their owne lear-ning, and vilified Believers in Christ for want thereof, say-ing, *Doe any of the Rulers, or of the Pharisees believe in him? but this people which know not the Law are cursed,* John 7.47. 48.49.

First, a company of fourty persons, or twenty, or lesse, is *To 14.* not such a small company, but they may be a Church pro-perly and truely so called, if there be nothing against them but this, *that such a number may seeme not sufficient:* We do not finde that God doth any where say, they must be above fourty, or else they cannot be a Church; and therefore no mortall man can justly say it: Nay, rather that speech of Christ, of *two or three gathered together in his name,* Matth. 18.20. doth plainly imply that if there be a greater number then two or three, whom they being not satisfied in the an-swere of an offendor may appeale unto, and in so doing tell the Church, such a small number may be a Church, and may have the blessing of his presence to be among them. Besides, the time hath been, in the dayes of *Adam* and *No-ah,* when there was not fourty persons in the world, and yet *Adams* family in his time, and *Noah* in his, was in those dayes a Church, if there was any Church on earth. And if Christ and his twelve Disciples were the first Chri-stian Church, it is too much for any man to say, that twen-ty or fourty is such a small company that they cannot be a Church.

Secondly, for the matter of Government, there is a diffe-rence betweene ability and right: In respect of the former, in as much as ſome caſes are more difficult then others, and ſome Churches of leſſe ſpirituall abilities then others, and God doth not afford aſſiſtance and direction at ſome times ſo much as at others ; therefore in ſuch caſes it is requiſite that Churches ſhould ſeeke for light, and counſell, and advice, from other Churches : as the Church at *Antioch* did ſend unto the Church at *Ieruſalem* in a Queſtion, which could not bee determined among themſelves, *Act.* 15.2. But this is not becauſe they have no right, but when they are not able.

Thirdly, as for right, let it be conſidered how the Church at *Antioch* did long endeavour to have ended that matter amongſt themſelves, before they determined to ſend to *Ieruſalem*, verſ.2. which ſhewes that they had power or right to have tranſacted that buſineſſe among themſelves, if ability had ſerved ; or otherwiſe, that endeavour had been ſinfull, as being a preſuming to doe that, whereunto they had no right. We conceive then that every Church, properly ſo called, though they be not above fourty, or twenty perſons, or ten, or the leaſt number that you mention, have right and power from Chriſt to tranſact all their owne Eccleſiaſticall buſineſſes among themſelves, if ſo be they be able, and carry matters juſtly, and according to the Rules of the Word. The power of the Keyes, *Matth.16.19.* among other things noteth Miniſteriall or delegated power of Government ; and this power is committed by Chriſt unto the Church, as may appeare, if wee conſider, firſt, to whom Chriſt directed his Speech in that place of Scripture ; not to *Peter* alone, but to all the Diſciples alſo, for to them all the Queſtion was propounded by Chriſt, *verſ.*15. And *Peter* anſwered in all their names.

Secondly, that he and they were not then looked upon as Apoſtles, or generall officers of all Churches (for that Commiſſion was not yet given them) but as Diſciples and Beleevers, believing with the heart, and confeſſing with the mouth Jeſus Chriſt, the rocke upon whom the Church is built ; wherein as they did repreſent all Believers, ſo in *Peter* and the reſt, the Keyes are committed to all Believers that ſhall joine together in the ſame confeſſion, according
to

to the order and ordinance of Christ. And therefore afterward this power of Government is expressly given to the
Church, *Matth.*18.17. according hereunto in that description
tion of the visible Church, as it is instituted by Christ in
the new Testament, *Rev.*4. The members of the Church
are seene by *John* in a vision sitting on thrones, cloathed
with white rayment, having on their heads Crownes of
Gold, *ver.*14. Now Thrones and Crownes are ensignes of
authority and power, to note unto us that authority and
governing power, which is committed by Christ unto the
Church. Doctor *Fulke* hath this saying ; *The Keyes of the
Kingdome of Heaven (whatsoever they are) be committed to the
whole Church, and not to one person onely, as Cyprian, Augustine,
Chrysostome, Jerome, and all the ancient Doctors (agreeably to the
Scriptures) doe confesse, against the Popes pardons* chap.3. P.381.
And elsewhere he saith ; The authority of Excommunication pertaineth to the whole Church, although the
judgement and execution thereof is to be referred to the
Governours of the Church ; which exercise that authority,
as in the name of Christ, so in the name of the whole
Church whereof they are appointed Governours, to avoid
confusion : against the *Rhemists* on 1 *Cor.*5.*Sect* 3.

And Doctor *Whitaker* hath these words : *Hoc est quod nos
dicimus Petrum gessisse personam omnium Apostolorum; quare hanc
promissionem non uni Petro, sed toti Ecclesiæ factam esse, & totam
Ecclesiam in illo claves accepisse. De pontif.Roman.Q.2 c.4 Sect.*
17. And in that Booke hee is pregnant and plaine in this,
that by the Keyes is meant all Ecclesiasticall power and
Jurisdiction, and that these Keyes are given in *Peter* to the
whole Church : The same is also taught by Master *Parker
Polit.Eccles.l.3 c.1.2.3.4.5.6.* where he proves by many Arguments, that every visible Church (which hee acknowledgeth to be no other but a particular congregation) hath
the power of all Ecclesiasticall Government and Jurisdiction committed to it by Christ Jesus ; and answereth many
Objections to the contrary : And page 2 of that third Book,
making mention of foure Opinions concerning those
words of the Keyes, and power of binding and loosing

F 3   *Matth.*

*Matth.*16.19. the firſt of them that underſtand the Pope onely to be meant thereby, as *Peters* ſucceſſour : the ſecond of them that underſtand it of the Diocelan Biſhop : The third of them that underſtand thoſe words as meant of the Miniſters, but the Miniſters alone : The fourth of them that underſtand *Peter* to repreſent the Church in that place, and therefore that that promiſe is made unto the Church : Of theſe he refuſeth the three firſt as unſound, and maintaines the fourth as onely agreeing to the truth. And Maſter *Bayne* ſaith, Every Church by Chriſts inſtitution hath power of Government, *Dioceſ. Tryall Queſt.* 1.*p.* 8. And hee tells us page 11. what hee meant by Church : The word Church (ſaith he) wee underſtand here not figuratively tataken Metonymically for the place, Synecdochecally for Miniſters adminiſtring ordinances ; but properly, for a body politicke ſtanding of People to be taught and governed, and of Teachers and Governours : So that in his judgement every Church (properly ſo called) hath power of Government within it ſelfe : and by theſe words of his it may alſo be concluded, that all power of Government is not in the Elders alone, for the power of Government by Church inſtitution is in every Church properly ſo called ; But Miniſters are not a Church in propriety of ſpeech, but onely figuratively by a ſynecdoche ; And therefore all power of Government is not in the Miniſters alone, but a Church properly ſo called is the Body politique, conſiſting of people and Miniſters : But of this more may bee ſaid in the next Queſtion.

    Fourthly for the matters of Independency, whereof this *Queſtion* alſo makes mention : We doe confeſſe the Church is not ſo independent but that it ought to depend on Chriſt both for direction from the rules of his holy Word, *Ioh.* 10. 27. *Act.* 3. 23. and for the aſſiſtance of his holy Spirit, to diſcerne thoſe rules, and to walke according to them when they ſhall be diſcerned, *Ioh.* 15. 5. and 16. 13. but for dependency upon men, or other Churches, or other ſubordination unto them in regard of Church Government or power, Wee know not of any ſuch appointed by Chriſt in his Word. Our Saviours words are plaine, *If a man heare not the*

the Chu ch, let him be to thee as an Heathen *or* Publican. And his promise unto his Church is plaine also, that *whatsoever they shall binde on earth, shall be bound in Heaven, &c.* Mat. 18. 17. &c. And the Apostle bids the Church deliver the impenitent sinner unto *Satan,* 1 *Cor.* 5. 4.5.6. Now when the man upon the Churches censure comes to be in case as an *Heathen* or *Publican,* yea becomes bound in Heaven as well as bound in earth, and also delivered unto *Satan,* this seems to us to be such a firme ratification of the Churches censure, as leaves no roome for any other Ecclesiasticall power on earth to reverse or disanull the same, and so takes away that kinde of dependency and subordination of Churches. *Nos plane dicimus Ecclesias initiò regi solitas esse à suis pastoribus, sic quidem ut nullis essent externis, aut Ecclesijs, aut Episcopis subditæ, non Colossensis, Ephasina, non Philippensis, Thessaloniensi, non kæ Romanæ, non Romana cuiquam, sed paris omnes inter se juris essent, id est, sui omnes juris et mancipij* Whitak. *de Pontif. Roman.* Question 1. Chapter 1. Section 3. That is in summe. The Churches were not dependent and subordinate to others, but all of them absolutely free, and independent. Wee affirme saith Master *Baine,* that all Churches were singular Congregations equall in dependent each of other in regard of subjection, Diocesse tryall. *Q* 1. *pag* 13. The twentieth Chapter of Mr. *Parker* his third Booke of *Eccles. Politie,* hath this Title De *summitate Ecclesiæ particularis.* And the Title of the 21. is, *De paritate Ecclesiarum* where he openeth and explaineth, and by many Arguments and Testimonies confirmeth what we hold of the independency and paritie of Churches, to which learned discourse of his, we referre you for further satisfaction in this point.

To 15.

Wee doe believe that Christ hath ordained that there should be a Presbytery or Eldership, 1 *Tim.* 4. 14. And that in every Church. *Tit.* 1. 5. *Acts* 14. 23. 1 *Cor.* 12. 28. whose worke is to teach and rule the Church by the Word and lawes of Christ, 1 *Tim.* 5. 17. and unto whom so teaching and ruling all the people ought to be obedient and submit themselves, *Heb.* 13. 17. And therefore a Government meerly Popular or Democraticall (which Divines and Ortho-

thodox Writers doe fo much condemne in *Morillius,* and
fuch like) is farre from the practice of thefe Churches, and
we believe faire from the minde of **Chrift.**

Secondly, neverthelefle a Government meerely Arifto-
cratical, wherein the Church government is fo in the hands
of fome *Elders,* as that the reft of the body are wholly excluded from entermedling by way of power therein, fuch a
government we conceive alfo to be without Warrant of the
Word, and likewife to be injurious to the people, as infrin-
ging that liberty which Chrift hath given to them in choo-
fing their owne Officers, in admitting of Members, and
cenfuring of offendors, even Minifters themfelves when
they be fuch; as the Church of *Coloffe* muft admonifh *Ar-*
chippus of his duety, *Col.* 4. 17. Mafter *Parker* you know hath
22. Arguments to prove the fuperiority of the Churches
over and above her officers, *Polit. Ecclef. lib.3. cap.12.* And
Mafter *Barne* faith, If the Church have power by election
to choofe a Minifter, and fo power of inftituting him, then
of deftituting alfo: *Inftituere & deftituere ejufdem eft poteftatis,*
Diocef. Triall P.88. And againe no reafon evinceth the
Pope, though a generall Paftors fubject to the cenfure of
a Church occumenicall, but the fame proveth a Diocefan
Bifhop, (and wee may adde, and a Congregationall Minifter) fubject to the cenfure of the particular Church, *pag.*
89. And whereas it might be objected, then may Sheep cenfure the Shepherd, Children their fathers, which were ab-
furd. To this he anfwereth, that fimilitudes hold not in
all things, naturall Parents are no waies Children, nor in
ftate of fubjection to their Children: but fpirituall fathers are fo fathers, that in fome refpects they are children
to the whole Church. So Shepherds are no waies Sheep but
Minifters are in regard of the whole Church. 2. Parents
and Shepherds are abfolutely Parents and Shepherds, bee
they good or evill, but fpirituall Parents and Paftors are
no longer fo, then they do accordingly behave themfelves
p. 89. (To the fame purpofe and more at large is this Objection anfwered by Mafter *Parker. Polit. Ecclef. l.* 3. *c.* 12.
p 78 79. And againe, if their owne Churches have no
power over them, it will be hard to fhew wherein others
have

have such power of Jurisdiction over persons who belong
not to their owne Churches, *p.* 89. So that all power is not
in the Officers alone, seeing the Officers themselves, if they
offend, are under the power of the Church. Even *Paul* himselfe though an extraordinary Officer, yet would not take
upon him to excommunicate the incestuous person, without
the Church, but sends to them exhorting them to doe it; and
blames them because they had not done it sooner, 1 *Cor.* 5.
which shewes that the exercise of all Church power of government, is not in the Officers alone: And therefore the
Lord *Iesus* reproving *Pergamus* and *Thyatira* for suffering
Balaamites, Nicholaitans, and the woman *Iezebel* among them,
and calling on them for reformation herein, *Rev.* 2. sends
his Epistle, not onely to the Angels of those Churches, but
also to the Churches, or whole Congregations, as appeareth
Rev. 1.11. And also in the conclusion of those Epistle, where
the words are, let him that hath an eare heare what the spirit saith, (not onely to the Angels) but unto the Churches;
whereby it appeares, that the suffering of these corrupt persons and practises, was the sinne of the whole Church, and
the reforming of them, a duty required of them all. Now
the reforming of abuses in the Church, argues some exercise of Church government, as the suffering of them argues some remisseness therein; and therefore it followes,
that some exercise of Church government was required of
the whole Church and not all of the Angels alone. Sure it
is the whole Congregation of *Israel* thought it their duty
to see to the reforming of abuses, when they appeared to
spring up amongst them, as appeareth by their behaviour &
practise when the two Tribes and an halfe had set up the
Altar upon the bankes of *Jordan, Ios.* 22. for it is said, that
the whole Congregation of the Children of *Israel* gathered
themselves together at *Shilo,* to go up to warre against them,
v. 12. And when *Phineas* and ten Princes with him, were
sent to expostulate with them about the matter, it was the
whole Congregation that sent them, *v.* 13. 14. And when
they delivered their Message they spake in the name of the
whole Congregation, saying, Thus saith the whole congregation of the Lord, what trespasse is this? &c. *v.* 16.

G   which

which plainely declares, that the whole congregation (and not the Elders or Rulers alone) thought it their duty to fee abufes reformed and redreffed, which could not be without fome exercife of government. And when *Achan* the Sonne of *Carmi* had committed a trefpaffe in theaccurfed thing, *Iof.* 7. it is counted the finne of the whole congregation and fuch a finne as brought a Plague upon them all: for it is faid the children of *Ifrael* committed a trefpaffe in the accurfed thing, *v.* 1. And God faith to *Iofhua* (not the El ers have finned, but) *Ifrael* hath finned, and they have tranfgreffed my Covenant, and they have ftolne of the accurfed thing, and put it among their owne ftuffe. *v.* 11. And for this, wrath fell on all the congregation of *Ifrael* and that man perifhed not alone in his iniquity, *Iofh.* 22. 20. Now why fhould not he have perifhed alone, but wrath muft fall upon them all? and why fhould his finne, be the finne of all the congregation, if the care of preventing it, and timely fuppreffing the fame, (which could not be without fome exercife of Church government) had not bin a duty lying upon all the whole congregation, but upon the Elders and Officers alone? doubtleffe the juft Lord, who faith, every man fhall beare his owne burden, *Gal.* 6. 5. would not have brought wrath upon all the congregation for *Achans* finne, if fuch government as might have prevented, or timely reformed the fame, had not belonged to the whole congregation, but to the *Elders* alone. And before this time all the children of *Ifrael* (and not the *Elders* alone) are commanded to put Lepers and uncleane perfons out of the Campe. *Numb.* 5. 1, 2. By all which it appeareth, that all exercife of Church Government is not in the *Elders* alone, but fome power is in the people.

And elfe-where he counts it no Sacriledge for Members of the Church, though not in office, to handle thofe keyes, *Mat.* 16. but rather a frivolous thing to thinke otherwife; *Quafi abfque facrilegio*, faith he, *tractare claves privati nequeant, qui eas privatim tractare iubentur. Quoties fratres fuos admonere, confolari, et ædificare. Imò verò eft & publica clavium tractatio quam plebs Chriftiana in unum coacta fine ullo facrilegio miniftrat,* 1 Cor. 5. *Polit. Ecclef. l.* 3. *c.* 2. *p.* 8. And yet this is not a
                                                                singular

singular conceit of his or ours, but the concurrent judgement of many worthy witnesses of the truth in these latter dayes, who do with great consent hold the Ecclesiasticall governmen to be of a mixt form compounded of all three Estates, and that the people are not to be wholly excluded " from having any thing to do therein. *Si velimus Christum* " *ipsum respicere, fuit semper Ecclesia Regimen monarchicum: Si* " *Ecclesia presbyteros, qui in Doctrina et disciplina suas partes* " *agebant, Aristocraticum: si totum corpus Ecclesie quatenus in Ele-* " *Ctione Episcoporum et presbyterorum suffragia ferebat, ita tamen* " *ut ἰνταξία semper à presbyteris servaretur, Democraticum: Sic* " *partim Aristocritum partim Democraticum, partim etiam Monar-* " *chicum est, semperque fuit Ecclesia Regimen,* Whita. *de pontif.* " Rom. Qu. 1. c. 1. *sect.* 2. The Church (saith Mr. Cart- " *wright*) is governed with that kinde of Government, " which the Philosophers that write of the best Com- " mon-wealths affirme to be the best. For in respect of " Christ the head it is a Monarchy, and in respect of the " Ancients and Pastors that Governe in Common, and " with like Authority among themselves, it is an Aristo- " craty, or rule of the best men; and in respect that the peo- " ple are not secluded, but have their interest in Church " matters, it is a Democraty, or popular State, 1 *Reply p.* 51. And when Dr. *Whitegift,* from the Doctrine of the Authors of the Admonition would infer this consequence, *viz.* that then the more that ruled the better estate it should be, and so the popular state should be the best: In Answer " hereunto he saith, I have spoken of this before, where I " declared that the mixed estate is best, both by the exam- " ple of the Kingdome of Christ and also of this our " Realme, *pag.* 181. 182. And againe, whereas Mr. Dr. " saith, that Excommunication, and consequently Absolu- " tion or restoring to the Church again pertaineth only to " the Minister: it remaineth that I shew that the *Presbytery* " or *Eldership* and the whole *Church* also, hath interest in the " excommunication and consequently in the absolution or " restoring unto the Church againe, *p.* 183. And " againe, it is certaine Saint *Paul* did both understand and " observe the rule of our Saviour Christ (*viz* that rule,

" *Mat.* 18. *Tell the Church*) but he communicateth this
" power of Excommunication with the Church : and
" therefore it muſt needs be the meaning of our Saviour
' Chriſt, that the Excommunication ſhould be by many,
" and not by one, and by the Church, and not by the Mi-
" niſter of the Church alone, for hee biddeth the Church
" of *Corinth* twiſe in the firſt Epiſtle, once by a Metaphor,
" another time in plaine words, that they ſhould Excom-
" municate the Inceſtuous perſon. And in the 2d. Epiſtle,
' underſtanding of the Repentance of the man, he intreat-
" eth them that they would receive him again: And ther-
" fore conſidering that the Abſolution of the Excommu-
" nication doth pertain unto the *Churches,* it followeth that
" the excommunication doth in like manner appertaine unto
" it. *p.*184. And again that the Ancients had the ordering of
" theſe things, and that the peoples conſent was required,
" & that the *Miniſters* did not take upon them of their own
" Authority to Excommunicate, &c. It may appeare al-
" moſt in every page of *Cyprians Epiſtles.* In *Auguſtines* time
" it appeareth alſo, that that conſent of the Church was
" required, *p.*187.

To theſe may be added, Mr. *Fenner,* who ſpeaking of the
Eccleſiaſticall Preſbytery, and of the buſineſſe which the
Preſbytery is to deale in, which hee diſtinguiſheth into ju-
diciarie, as deciding of doubts, and diſpencing of Cenſures,
and extrajudiciary, as Election, Ordination &c. hath theſe
words, *Atque hæc ſunt negotia quæ præſtari debent: In quibus per
omnes Eccleſias ſumma Eccleſiaſtica poteſtas presbyterio demandata
eſt, ita tamen ut in his quæ maximi ſunt momenti, et ad eccleſiæ totius
bonum vel ruinam maxime ſpectant, poſt πρεβ λευσι ſuam de his cap-
tum conſilia Eccleſiæ denunciantur, ut ſi quid habeant quod conſulant
vel objiciant in medium proferant : poſtea, autem auditis et aſſenti-
en ibus (niſi ad majorem Senatum negotium deferri fuerit, neceſſe ad
turbas vitandas ſive componendas, quod tum cum Major pars Eccleſiæ diſſentit, faciendum eſt) decervenda et pro decretis Eccleſiis pro-
ponenda ſunt,* and then he declares what hee meanes by thoſe
matters *maximi momenti, viz.* excommunication, abſolution,
elections, and depoſings of *Miniſters,* and ſuch like, *Sacra The.
l.b.* 7. *c* 7. wherin he plainly ſheweth, that though the power
of

of the Presbytery be very great yet in things ofgreatest mo-
ment, as Censures and Elections, the people if they have
any thing to counsell or object, have liberty to bring it in;
and afterwards matters are to be concluded when they have
bin heard speake, and have given their consent, for which
liberty and power of the people he bringeth these Scriptures, 2 *Chro.* 30. 23. *Acts* 1. 15. 23. 26. 1 *Cor.* 5. 4. & 2 *Cor.*
1. 6. 7. *Zanchius* speaking of that Question, *per quos exerceri debet excommunicatio,* answers thus, *nempe per Ecclesiam,
seu per ministros Ecclesiæ nomine, eoque et cum consensu totius Ecclesiæ Promissio illa, Quæcunq; ligaveritis, ad totam Ecclesiam est
facta,* Ergo &c. *Præterea Apostolus hoc expressius declaravit,
1 Cor. 5. congregatis vobis, &c. alloquebatur autem totam Ecclesiam. Patres idem docent: Cyprianus ad Cornelium Rom. Episcopum scribit se multum laborasse apud plebem, ut par daretur lapsis
pænitentibus: Si ergo non erat unius Episcopi cum suo Presbyterio
solvere quempiam, sed requirebatur plebis eoque totius Ecclesiæ
consensus: Ergo neque ligari quispiam poterat, id est Excommunicari, sine totius Ecclesiæ consensu. Augustinus etiam contra Donati-
stas ait, supersedendum esse excommunicatione Quando tota plebs
laborant eodem morbo, Quid ita? causam adfert, Quia inquit, non
assentientur excommunicationi, &c. Satis aperte docet tunc tem-
poris non solitum fuisse excommunicationem ferri in Quempiam sine
totius Ecclesiæ consensu; et ratio est in promptu, Quæ enim ad omnes pertinent cum consensu omnium fieri debent: Ergo sine totius
Ecclesiæ consensu excommunicari nemo debet.* And then com-
paring the Government of the Church, to the Roman
Common-wealth which had the Dictators, the Senate and
the Quirites, and shewing that the Church government in
respect of Christ is a Monarchy in respect of the Presbyters
an Aristocratie, and in respect of the people a Democratie,
he concludes thus, *In rebus igitur gravissimis, quæ ad totum
corpus pertinent, uti est Excommunicatio, sine consensu et authoritate
totius Ecclesiæ nihil fieri debet, de Redempt. in præ c. 1. pag. 983. &c.*
Calvins words are these, *Cyprianus cum meminit per quos suo
tempore exerceretur (viz. potestas jurisdictionis) adjungere solet
totum Clerum Episcopo, sed alibi quoque demonstrat, sic præfuisse clerum ipsum, ut plebs interim à cognitione non excluderetur, sic enim
scribit; Ab initio Episcopatus mei statui sine Cleri consilio & plebis*
consensu

consensu nihil agere, Instit.1.4.c.11.Sect.6. And againe, *Hoc addo, illam esse legitimam in excommunicando homine progressionem quam demonstrat Paulus, si non soli Seniores seorsim id faciant, sed conscia & approbante Ecclesia, in eum scilicet modum, ut plebis multitudo non regat actionem, sed observet, ut testis & custos, ne quid per libidinem à paucis geratur, Instit.l.4.c.12.Sect.7.*

Those Ministers that penned the Christian and modest offer of disputation, doe say, That the Pastor and Elders that exercise Ecclesiasticall Jurisdiction, ought not to performe any maine and materiall Ecclesiasticall act, without the free consent of the congregation, in Propos.8.

The Refuter of Doctor *Downams* Sermon for the superiority of Diocesan Bishops, is plaine and full also in this point, in *Part 2.* of his reply *p.104 105,106.* where answering Doctor *Downam,* that counted it schismaticall novelty, that the forme of the Church Government should be holden in part to be Democratticall, and that his Refuter for so holding was a *Brownist* or *Anabaptist*; he not onely proves the power of the people from the Scripture, and delivers his owne judgement, that the Ecclesiasticall Government is of a mixt forme, compounded of all three Estates; but for the same tenent, and that the Church government is in part Democraticall or popular, he alledgeth the testimonies of the Centuries, of *Illyricus,* of Doctor *Fulke.* Doctor *Willet, Cyprian, Augustine, P.Martyr,* Dr *Whitaker,* and others: Master *Baines* his judgement we heard before in the former Question. *Vrsinus* speaking of that Question *Quibus commissa est potestas clavium,* hath these words: *Quibus denunciatio verbi divini delegata est, iisdem & potestas illa clavium: qua verò denunciatio fit in Ecclesiastica disciplina est totius Eccles ad totam enim Ecclesiam pertinet disciplina & jurisdictio spiritualis, sed alio modo fit illa denunciatio in verbi divini ministerio, quam in Ecclesia judicio.* And then telling how this denunciation is done in the Ministery, and by the Ministers of the Word, he comes to declare how it is done in Church censures: *In Ecclesiastico judicio* (saith he) *gratia & ira Dei non fit denunciati ab uno aliquo privatim sed à tota Ecclesia cui nomine totius Ecclesiæ ab iis qui ad hoc delecti sunt communi omnium consensu.* And a little after answering objections brought against the
use

use of Excommunication, he hath these words: *Potest concedi quod Christus non intelligat Presbyterium (viz.*in that place *Matth.18. Tell the Church) sed proprie sumat vocabulum Ecclesia ante Christum Judaica, post Christum Christiana: Sed in Ecclesia jurisdictione oportet aliquem esse ordinem, aliquos oportet esse constitutos ab Ecclesia, alioquin esset αταξία.* And speaking of that Question, *Quis ordo servari debeat in exercenda clavium potestate* (he saith) *principalis pars in excommunicatione est denunciatio, qua &c. atque haec denunciatio qua quis excommunicatur non est penes Ministrum Ecclesiae, sed penes ipsam Ecclesiam, & ejus nomine fit, quia mandatum hoc à Christo datum est Ecclesia; nam ipse ait expresse, Dic Ecclesiae.* And finally, speaking of abuses to be avoided, and cautions to be observed in Excommunication, he hath such words in the fourth Proposition, or Rule there annext, as doe declare it to be his judgement that if Excommunication should be passed by a few, without the consent of the whole Church, such proceedings would be both Oligarchy and Tyranny: *Attentem expendatum* (saith he) *à toto Presbyterio, probetur ab Ecclesia, non suscipiatur privata authoritate, ne ministerium Ecclesia convertatur in ὀλιγαρχίαν & Tyrannidem*, in his Comment upon the Catechisme, in the place *De clavibus regni coelorum.*

Pareus delivering certaine *porismata* or, conclusions concerning Excommunication, hath this for the fifth of them, *Quòd excommunicandi potestas non sit penes unum Episcopum, vel paucos pastores, sed penes Ecclesiam; proinde licet pastores & presbyteri ordinis causâ primas habeant partes circa censuras Ecclesiasticas, & per eos hac administrentu; quod tamen citra consensum Ecclesia pastores ad exclusionem procedere non debeant, alibi demonst. avimus in 1 Cor.5.* And a little after, answering *Stapletons* objections that would have the power of Excommunication to be in the Bishop-alone he brings in the case of *Cyprian,* who could not absolve the *Lapsi* without the people : *Cyprianus* (saith hee) *ad Cornelium Romanum Episcopum scribit se multum apud plebem laborasse ut pax daretur lapsis, quam si per se dare potuisset, non erat cur adeo in persuadenda plebe se fatigasset.* So that in the judgement of *Pareus* and *Cyprian* all power of Church government was not in the Presbyters,
but

but some power was in the people.

Musculus, although he thinke there be little ufe of Excommunication and Church difcipline, where there is a
Chriftian Magiftrate, yet when it is to be ufed, he would
not have the people excluded from having any hand therein, as may appeare by thofe words of his, where he fpeakes
*De difciplina Ecclefiaftica : Hifce de rebus non conftituet Minifter
fuo proprio arbitratu, fed erit ad inftitutionem earum director, & ad-
hibebit fuffragia & confenfum fuæ plebis, ne quicquam invitæ Ecclefiæ imponatur. Denique curabit ut plebs ipfa viros graves, ti-
mentes Dei, ac boni teftimonii deligat, quorum curâ & vigilantiâ
difciplina Ecclefiaftica adminiftratur, & fi quid gravioris momenti
accidat, ad ipfam Ecclefiam referatur: Loc.com.de Miniftris verbi
Dei, in tit.de poteftate Miniftrorum p.377.* And afterward, in
the latter end of that place, comming to fpeake of the depo-
fing of unworthy Minifters, he hath thefe words : *Quæritur
hic per quos difciplina ifta adminiftrari debeat ? Refpondeo, primum
Ecclefiæ populus poteftatem habens elegendi dignum Miniftrum,
habet etiam (tefte Cypriano) poteftatem indignum recufandi : de-
inde qui Judices funt Cenforefque morum in Ecclefia ex officio te-
nentur redarguere peccantem Miniftrum, fi duobus aut tribus te-
ftibus fide dignis coram Ecclefia Dei convictus fuerit. Tertiò, iidem cum confenfu & fuffragiis plebis deponent Miniftrum, vel ad
tempus, vel in univerfum, vel excommunicabunt tandem juxta qua-
litatem peccati vel defectus illius,* p.429. Doctor *Ames* faith,
Poteftas hujus difciplinæ (viz. of Excommunication) *quoad
jus ipfum pertinet ad Ecclefiam illam in communi, cujus membrum
eft peccator: ad illos enim pertinet ejicere, ad quos pertinet primò
admittere, & corporis totius intereft ex æquo membrorum confervæ-
tio vel amputatio, cum Ecclefiæ idcirco confenfu (eoque Magi-
ftratu non permittente tantum, fed & approbante & conftituente) eft
executioni mandanda.* Medul.Theol.l.1.c.37.Sect.26.

Laftly, Mafter *Parker* obferving a diftinction betweene
power, and the difpencing of power; that the one is in the
Church and the other in the Presbyters, hath thefe words:
*Neque tamen difpenfatio omnis, omneqre exercitum eft penes recto-
res folos, fed juxta temperamentum forma partim Ariftocraticæ,
partim Democraticæ de mandata Rectoribus fuis Ecclef, quæ ipfa
per fe obire fatis commodè nequit, retinente vero difpenfationem illam*

Iam illudque exercitium quod & ipsi convenit, & pertinet ad ejus dignitatem, authoritatem, & libertatem a Christo donatam. Posit. Eccles.l.3.c.7. And elsewhere he saith, *Imo vero est & publica clavium tractatio, quam plebes Christiana in unum coacta, sine ullo sacrilegio administrat.* Polit.Eccles.l.3 c.2 p.8.

These testimonies we thought good to produce in this Question, lest any should thinke that to give any Church power of Government to the people, were some singular opinion of ours, swerving from the truth, and disallowed by Orthodox Writers of the Reformed Churches; and no doubt but besides these here cited, the same is taught by others also, whom now we spare to alledge, intending onely these few for a taste instead of many.

2. And therefore when this Question demandeth whether we give the exercise of all Church power of government to the whole Congregation, or to the *Presbyters* thereof alone ? Our Answer is, neither thus nor so, neither all to the people excluding the Presbytery, nor all to the Presbytery excluding the People. For this were to make the government of the Church either meerly Democraticall, or meerly Aristocraticall, neither of which we believe it ought to be.

3. Whereas this Question demandeth to know what acts of Government the Presbyters may doe more then any other may doe, and to have those particular acts mentioned: this seemeth to us to be a very large demand, for who is able to mention all the particular acts of government, which any one Governour may performe in his time, especially if he continue long in his place ? But if your meaning in this Point be not of the Individualls, but of the species or kinds, yet even there also it is much to require the particular mentioning of all; yet to give you a taste take these. The calling of Assemblies and dismissing of the same againe; The ordinary preaching of the Word, which is done by way of Office; and being the peoples mouth unto God in Prayer; The dispensing of Baptisme, and the Lords Supper: The permitting of any to speak in an orderly way; and againe enjoining silence: The putting of matters to Vote, and pronouncing of sentence in the censure of offendors, or re-

ceiving in of Penitents after their fall, and blessing of the
people in the name of the Lord; These are Acts of Church
Government, which the Presbyters may doe according to
the Word, and another member may not do without breach
of Order and presuming above his place.

4. It is also here demanded, what the Presbyters may do
without the particular consent of the rest? To which wee
answer, that when they doe what the Lord Christ (whose
Stewards they are) by his word requires of them in their
places, this should not be without the consent of the rest,
for the rest of the Church ought to consent thereto: Christs
Sheep ought to heare his voice, *Iohn* 10. 27. and to obey them
that speak unto them in his name, *Heb.* 13. 17. And if any
man should in such case willfully dissent, the Church ought
to deale with such an one, for not consenting to the will
and waies of Christ, or else they shall all be guilty of the
sinfull dissent of such an one. So that this Passage (if it be
meant of Presbyters doing their duty) without the consent of the people, goes upon a supposall (in respect of the
people) of that which never ought to be, neither are wee
to suppose but that there may be rule when the *Elders* and
Brethren doe not dissent nor are divided one from another:
The multitude of them that believed in the first Christian
Church at *Ierusalem*, were of one heart and of one soule,
A l. 4. 32. Yet none needs to doubt, but there was rule and
Government amongst them, when yet their agreement was
such, that the Apostles and Elders did nothing without the
full consent of the rest. It is a miserable mistake either to
thinke that in the Church of Christ the Elders and Brethren must needs dissent one from another, or if they all
consent, that then there can be no ruling but against the
peoples minde. They were none of the best Shepheards to
their flocks unto whom the Lord saith, with force and ri-
gour have you ruled them, *Ezech.* 34. 4. As for doing any
thing in their places which the word of Christ, the Lord
and Master of the Church, commandeth not, nor alloweth
such things, they neither ought to do nor ought the Church
to consent unto them, if they should; for that were to make
themselves partakers of their Rulers sinnes, and so to bring
Judgement

Judgement upon them all, as when the Priests did wicked-
ly beare rule, and the people loved to have it so, *Ieremiah*
5. 31.

5. Laſtly, this Queſtion demandeth how, and over whom
in thoſe Acts of Government, which are done by the Elders more then by other Members, or without the conſent
of the reſt, the Presbyters doe rule in propriety of ſpeaking more then the reſt of the Congregation? wherein are
ſundry particulars.

1. How they rule? Whereunto wee anſwer, that neither the *Elders* nor the people doe rule with Lordly and
Princely rule, and Soveraigne authority and power; for
that is proper to Chriſt over his Church: who is the onely Lord, 1 *Cor.* 12. 5. And King and Lawgiver that is able
to ſave and to deſtroy, *Iſa.* 33. 23. *Pſal.* 2. *Luk.* 19. 27. *Jam.*
4. 12. *The Elders are forbidden to be Lords over Gods heritage,*
1 *Pet.* 5. 3. *Or to exerciſe authority as the Kings and Princes of
the earth doe*, Matth. 20. 25,26. Luk. 22. 25,26. They are not
ſo to rule, as to doe what themſelves pleaſe, but they muſt
do whatſoever *Chriſt* hath commanded, *Mat.* 28. 20. Mr.
Baine ſheweth from theſe words there are diverſities of Mi-
niſteries, but one Lord, 1 *Cor.* 12. 5. That it is contrary to
the Scripture that there ſhould be in the Church more
Lords then one: (and ſaith he) look as great Lords have in
their Houſes Miniſters of more and leſſe honour, from
the Steward to the Scullery, but no Lord-like or Maſterlike power in any beſides themſelves: So is it with Chriſt
and his Church, which is the Houſe of God, wherein hee
is the Lord, Apoſtles and others having more or leſſe honourable ſervices, but no Maſterlike power over the mea-
neſt of their fellow ſervants: On *Epheſ.* 1. 22. *p.* 395. and
elſewhere he ſaith no Miniſter of the Word hath any power but Miniſteriall in the Church, the power of the Apoſtles themſelves and *Evangeliſts* is called διακονία, Acts 20.
2 *Tim.* 4. Yea ſuch a ſervice as doth make the Miniſters having it ſo ſervants, that they are no way Lords; many Miniſters, one Lord; we preach Chriſt Ieſus the Lord; our ſelves
your ſervants for Ieſus ſake, *Dioceſ.* Tryall. *Q.* 2. *p.* 74.
The Elders are to rule as Stewards, *Mat.* 24. 45. *Luke* 12.

42. As Shepheards, *Act.* 20. 28. As Captaines, guides, leaders or overseers, by going before the People, and shewing them the word and way of the Lord, 1 *Tim.* 3. 1. 5. & 5. 17. 1 *Thes.* 5. 12. *Heb.* 13. 17.

2. How they rule more then the rest of the Congregation do? Whereto the Answer is, that this is more then the rest of the Congregation doe in these acts, even as acting is more then consenting, and as it is more to be a Steward over of the House then one of the household, or to be a guide or leader, then to be guided or led.

3. Over whom they doe rule? even over the whole Church in generall, and every Member in particular, even all the flocke over which the Holy Ghost hath made them overseers, *Act.* 20. 28. 1 *Pet.* 3. 2.

To 16.   The rule is expresse and plaine that women ought not to speake in the Church, but to be in silence. 1 *Cor.* 14. 34. 1 *Tim.* 2 11,12. And therefore they ought not to vote in Church matters; besides voting imports some kind of government, and authority and power: now it is not government and authority, but subjection and obedience which belongs unto women, by the rule, and so is the practice of women amongst us.

To 17.   Church matters ought not to be determined meerly by multitude or plurality of Votes, but by rules from the word of Christ, whose will, (and not the will either of the Major, or Minor part of men,) is the onely rule and Law for Churches, *Iam.* 4. 12. *Isa.* 33. 22. *Mat.* 23. 8,9. *Exod.* 23. 2. 21, 22. For our practice among us, the Major part of the Church, yea usually the whole Church doth consent and agree in one minde and one judgement, and so gives a joint unanimus Vote; and the rule requires it should be so *Rom.* 15. 6. and the example of the Primitive Apostolike Churches, where things were carried (nor meerly by the Major or Minor part, the rest dissenting, but) ὁμοθυμαδὸν, or with one accord, *Act.* 1. 14. & 2. 46. & 4. 24. & 5. 12. & 15. 25. So that in this sence, matters with us are carried according to the Vote of the Major part, that is, with the joint consent

ſent of the whole Church , but yet becauſe it is the minde
of Chriſt. But it may be your meaning is in this *Queſtion*
to take it for granted that the Churches will be divided in
their Votes,and to know what courſe we take at ſuch times:
But if Churches lay aſide their owne affections,and give at-
tendance to the rule, and be (as all Churches ought to be)
men of humble ſpirits, and ſincere , and withall depend on
Chriſt their head and King for guidance , in their worke,
we know no neceſsity of ſuch a ſuppoſall , that they muſt
needs be divided in their votes, eſpecially conſidering what
promiſes he hath made unto his Church,of godly concord
and agreement among themſelves , and of his owne gracious preſence in the midſt of them, *Ier.* 32. 39. *Zeph.* 3. 9.
Mat. 18. 20. which promiſes we believe are not in vaine.
Neverthelesſe,we deny not but through the corruptions &
diſtempers of men, ſome diſſention may ariſe for a time in
a true Church, as it was in the Church at *Corinth* : and if a-
ny ſuch thing fall out among us (which we bleſſe God is
not often)then before matters be put to the vote,our courſe
of proceeding is after this manner. If the Elders and Major
part of the Church conſent in one concluſion , yet if any
brother diſſent, he is patiently heard , and his alledgements
of Scripture or good reaſons are duely weighed : If it appeare that his judgement is according to the rule,the whole
Church will readily yeeld, though before they were otherwiſe minded. But if it appeare they who diſſ nt from the
Major part are factiouſly or partially carried,the reſt labour
to convince them of their error by the rule, if they yeeld,
the conſent of all comfortably concurreth in the matter; if
they ſtill continue obſtinate, they are admoniſhed , and ſo
ſtanding under cenſure,their vote is nullified. If they without obſtinate oppoſition of the reſt, doe diſſent ſtill, yet referre the matter to the judgement of the Major part of the
body they are not wont to proceed to ſentence(if the matter be weighty as in Excommunication) till the reaſons on
both ſides have bin duly pondered, and all brotherly means
have been uſed for mutuall information and conviction. If
the difference ſtill continue the ſentence (if the matter be
weighty) is ſtill demurred , even till other Churches have

been conſulted with , who in ſuch a caſe will ſend their El
ders to communicate their apprehenſions and light, which
they do not *pro imperio*,binding the Church to reſt in their
dictates.but by propounding their grounds from the Scripture. Theſe courſes with Gods preſence and bleſsing(which
uſually accompanieth his Ordinance) faithfully taken and
followed,will prevaile either to ſettle one unanimous conſent in the thing. or at leaſt to preſerve peace in the Church
by the diſſentors ſubmiſsion to the judgement of the Major part , though they ſee not light ſufficient to warrant
them to act in the buſineſſe : Such ſubjection is according
to the rule, *Epheſ.5. 21. 1 Pet.5.5*. If the Church or the
Elders ſhould refuſe the teſtimony of other Churches according to God, they will (after brotherly admonition and
due patient waiting) deny them the right hand of fellowſhip, till they ſhall give better evidence of their ſubjection
to the Goſpel of Chriſt. But thanks be to God we never
had occaſion of ſuch withdrawing communion of one
Church from another, though now and then (as need requireth) Churches ſend to other Churches for their counſell and advice.

To 18.   Meanes to preſerve the Churches in unitie and verity,
and to reforme any that may erre, thankes bee to God we
have ſundry. Firſt, the holy Scriptures, which are a perfect rule for Doctrine and practiſe, *2 Tim.3.15 16. 2 Pet.1.*
19. Pſal.19.7,8. Secondly, the Miniſtery appointed by
Chriſt, *viz.* of Paſtors, Teachers, Elders, and Deacons,
Epheſ.4.11,12. 1 Cor 12.28. 1 Tim.5.17.1 Tim.3.1,2. &c and
*verſ.*8. and in both theſe we have frequently holden forth
unto us the Commandement of God,wherein he requires
Churches to bee of one mind and one judgement in the
truth, *1 Cor.1.10. & 2. 13.11. Epheſ.4.3. & Phil.1.27. &*
2.1,2. and his promiſe to lead his people into all truth, and
holy agreement therein, *Jer.32.29. Iſa 11 6,7 &c. Zeph.3.9.*
Ioh.16.13. with many motives and Rules from Scripture
for continuing in the ſaid truth and love. Now Faith
makes uſe of theſe promiſes. and ſubmits to theſe precepts
and exhortations, and ſo both theſe being mixt with Faith
are

are profitable meanes by the blessing of God for that end
aforesaid, *Heb.*4.2. as these Churches have found by experience, for these yeares since our comming into this Countrey: And any other meanes sanctified of God for the aforesaid end, we hope we should be glad with thankfull hearts
to improve and make use of as the Lord shall help.

As for a Platforme of Doctrine and Discipline which
you mention, as one meanes hereunto, if thereby you
meane no more but a confession of Faith of the holy doctrine which is according to godlinesse, we know nothing
but it may be lawfull and expedient in some cases for any
particular person that hath received the gift to doe it ; or
any Church, or al the Churches in any Christian Common-wealth, to compile and set forth such a platforme.
The practise of those Churches, whose Confessions are
contained in that booke called *The harmony of Confessions*, as
also of Master *Robinson* at *Leiden*, and others of our Nation
in other parts in the *Low-countries*, who have published such
platformes, we see no reason to condemne or disallow : neither count we it unlawfull or inexpedient for any Church
or Churches, or person or persons in the countrey, upon
just occasion to doe the like.

But if your meaning be of a platforme to be imposed by
authority upon others, or our selves, as a binding Rule of
Faith and practice, so that all men must believe and walke
according to that platforme, without adding, altering, or
omitting, then we are doubtfull whether such platformes
be lawfull or expedient. For if the Doctrine contained
therein doe in any particular swerve from the Doctrine
contained in Scripture then the imposing of them is so far
forth unlawfull; and if they be according to it, then they
may seeme needlesse, in as much as the forme of wholesome words contained in Scripture is sufficient. Which
reason against such Platformes makes nothing against Sermons or Preaching, though Sermons must be according to
the Doctrine contained in Scripture, because Preaching is
an ordinance of God and therefore not needlesse; which
we cannot say of such Platformes. Besides, as they are not
necessary, so they may be a snare unto men, and a dangerous

rous temptation of attending more to the forme of Doctrine delivered from the authority of the Church, and the
imposers, then to the examining thereof according to the
Rule of Scripture; and so their faith may by this meanes
stand in the wisedome or will of man, rather then in the
power of God as if men had dominion over their faith;
which things ought not so to be, 1 *Cor.*2.5. & 2.1.*ver.* Christians have liberty from God to search the Scriptures, and
try all things, and hold fast that which is good, *Act.*17.11.
*Ioh.*5.39. 1 *Thess.*5.21. but the foresaid imposing of platformes and confessions compiled by men, doth seeme to
abridge them of that liberty; and if it be any meanes of
unity, yet it may be a dangerous hinderance of some verity
and degree of truth as binding men to rest in their former
apprehensions and knowledge, without liberty to better
their judgement in those points, and shutting the doore a-
gainst any further light which God may give to his best
servants, and most discerning, beyond what they saw at
first: And therefore we doubt such imposed platformes are
not lawfull, or at least wise not expedient.

The consociation of Churches into *Classes* and Synods
we hold to be lawfull, and in some cases necessary; as namely in things that are not peculiar to one Church, but common to them all: And likewise when a Church is not able
to end any matter that concernes onely themselves, then
they are to seeke for counsell and advice from neighbour
Churches; as the Church at *Antioch* did send unto the
Church at *Ierusalem*, *Acts* 15. 2. the ground and use of
Classes and Synods, with the limitations therein to be observed, is summarily laid downe by Doctor *Ames, Medul.
Theol.l* 1.*c.*39.*Sect.*27. unto whom we do wholly consent in
this matter.

But when you speake of doing no weighty matter without the consent and counsell of a *Classe*, we dare not so far
restraine the particular Churches as fearing this would be
to give the *Classes* an undue power and more then belongs
unto them by the Word; as being also an abridgment of
that power which Christ hath given to every particular
Church, to transact their owne matters (whether more or
                                                      lesse

leſſe weighty) among themſelves (if ſo be they be able) without ſuch neceſſary dependence upon *Claſſes,* as we have ſhewed before in anſwer to *Q.14.Sect.3.&4.* of that Anſwere. And Maſter *Parker* teſtiſieth, that in *Genevah,* and in the *Low-countries,* where they have ſome uſe of *Claſſes,* yet it cannot bee ſaid that their particular Congregations are *abſque poteſtate omni in rebus grandioribus, ut in excommunicatione;* the particular Churches are not without power in the more weighty matters, as in Excommunication, *Polit. Eccleſ.li.2.c.36.Sect.11.p.310.* And Maſter *Baine* ſheweth the ſame, ſaying, They have power of governing themſelves, but for greater edification voluntarily confederate, not to uſe or exerciſe their power but with mutuall communion, one asking the counſell and conſent of the other, *Dioceſ.Triall Q.1.p.21.* And a little after *Geneva* made his conſociation, not as if the prime Churches were imperfect, and to make one Church by this union; but becauſe though they were intire Churches, and had the power of Churches, yet they needed ſupport in exerciſing of it, *&c.* which is the very ſame that wee ſaid before in *Q.14 viz.* That all Churches have right of Government within themſelves, but ſome had need of counſell and advice of others, becauſe they are of leſſe ability to tranſact their owne matters of themſelves. And Maſter *Parker* in the ſame place afore alledged in the page immediately precedent, clearly ſheweth againſt Doctor *Downham,* Doctor *Sutcliffe,* and others, that thoſe particular Congregations which have Presbyters of their owne, with power within themſelves, are the moſt perfect, and are preciſely formed *juxta formam illam qua in verbo patefacta eſt,* according to that forme which is revealed in the Word; whereas others which have not the like are more defective and imperfect. And if this be ſo, then to binde Churches to do no weighty matters without the counſell and conſent of *Claſſes,* were to binde them to bee imperfect. And for Synods, if they have ſuch power that their determination ſhall binde the Churches to obedience (as you ſpeake) it is more then we yet underſtand. Indeed *Bellarmine* makes Biſhops in a Councell or Synod to be Judges; and that *ſtandum ſit eorum*

I

rum

rum fententiæ, quia ipſi ſic ſtatuerunt, quomodo ſtatur ſententiæ Prætoris in cauſis politicis ; that is, either to obey or ſuffer: *de Concil.& Eccleſ.l.1.c.18.* But the Orthodoxe Writers do not conſent to him therein ; for in their judgement the ſentence of a Councell or Synod is onely *inquiſitio quædam & dictio ſententiæ miniſtratoria & limitata, ita ut tantum valeat decretum Concilii quantum valeat ejus ratio*, as Doctor *Ames* hath it in his *Bellarminus enervatus*, upon that place of *Bellarmine* : that is, The ſentence of a Synod is onely a certaine enquiring and giving of ſentence by way of Miniſtery, and with limitation; ſo that the decree of the Councell hath ſo much force as there is force in the reaſon of it. And *Junius* expreſſeth it thus ; *Sententia Concilii per ſe ipſam ſuaſionis non coactionis eſt judicium miniſteriale, non authoritatem, per ſe neceſſitatemque adferens, Animadverſ.* upon *Bellarmine* in that place : that is, The ſentence of a Councell is of it ſelfe onely of advice, not of compulſion or conſtraint , and brings with it a judgement miniſteriall, not authority of it ſelfe nor neceſſity ; whereunto we doe wholly conſent. As for that clauſe in this Queſtion, *That the determination of a Synod ſhould binde if not to obedience, yet to peaceable ſuffering*, we know not what ſufferings thoſe ſhould be : for puniſhments in Purſe or Perſon, in reſpect of the body or outward man, are not to be inflicted by Synods, but by civill Magiſtrates ; and Church-cenſures of Excommunication, or the like, belong to the particular Church of which an offendor is a member, out of the communion whereof a man cannot be caſt, but onely by his owne **Church.**

To 19.   Onely **Chriſt** hath Authority to make Lawes for the government of each particular Church, and the Members thereof, and his lawes doe oblige all the Members, and may not be omitted without ſinne, *Jam.4.12. Iſa.33.22. Mat.23.8,9 10. ct.3.23.* But for particular Churches, they have no power to make Lawes for themſelves or their Members, but to obſerve and ſee all their Members obſerve thoſe Laws which Chriſt hath given and commanded *Mat. 28.20 Deut.33.3. Iohn 10.27.* If any Church ſhall preſume further, they goe beyond their Commiſſion, and in
                                                      ſuch

such case their Ecclesiasticall Lawes may be omitted without sinne, nay it would be sinne to be subject to them *Col.2.* 20. To walke after them, *Hof.5.* 11. to be such servants of men as not to stand fast in the liberty wherewith Christ hath made us free, 1 *or.7.23. Gal.5.1.*

The outward calling of a Minister consisteth properly *To* 20. and essentially in election by the people, as Doctor *Ames* sheweth, *Caf.Conf.l 4.c.25.Q.6.* And this election is so essentiall,that without it the Ministers calling (if you speak of an ordinary Church officer) is a nullity; And therefore *Mornay*, that learned noble man of *France*, approveth that saying of *Chryfoftome*, election by the people is so necessary, as that without it there is neither Altar, nor Church, nor Priest-hood, where (omitting other things) it appeares to be their judgement, that without election by the people, the Ministery is void; And *Mornay* addeth of his owne, concerning the Bishops amongst the Papists,that they were *nulla plane χειροτια, nulla proinde, χ ιρ οσια*, for the one presupposed the other, no Imposition seeing without election, in his booke of the Church, *c.11.p.375.* Yet sometimes the peoples acceptance and approbation afterward may supply the want of election at the first, as *Iacobs* after consent and acceptance of *Lea*, made her to be his wife,though hee chose her not at the first. And by this we hold the calling of many Ministers in *England* may be excused, who at first came into their places without the consent of the people.

If ordination by imposition of hands, were of the essence of a Ministers calling then in those Churches,where such ordination is not used, their Ministers should want a lawfull calling, which were an hard sentence again st many Ministers in *Scotland*, where (as is reported) this ordination is not thought necessary; and therefore used or omitted indifferently. Wee looke at Ordination by Imposition of hands, as a solemne investing of men in o their places, whereto they have right and calling by election, like to the inauguration of a Magistrate in the Common-wealth, yet necessary by divine Institution. 1 *Tim.4.14.* But not so necessary as if the Ministers calling were a nullity without it. *Essentia ipsa vocationis, in electione legitima consistit; Ordinatio pendet ab electione, sicut Coronatio Principis, aut Magistratus inauguratio, ab electione, successione, aut aquivalente aliqua constitutione. Ames Bellarm. enervat. Lib. 3. de clericis, c. 2. Sect. 3.* That is, the essence of a Ministers calling consists in lawfull election, Ordination depends upon Election, as the Coronation of a Prince, or the Inauguration of a Magistrate, depends upon Election, Succession, or some other Constitution æquivalent. And againe, *Ritus impositionis manuum non est absolute necessarius ad esse Pastoris, non magis quam Coronatio ad esse Regis, aut celebratio nuptiarum ad earum esse. sect.* 10. That is, the right of Imposition of hands is not absolutely necessary to the essence of a Pastor, no more then the Coronation to the essence of a King, or the Celebration of Marriage to the essence thereof.

To 21. Ordination of Ministers is not a private action but publique, and ought to be done publiquely in the Assembly of the Church, and therefore the persons that performe it, (whether they be ordinary Church Officers or no) cannot in any congruity of speech be called meere private persons in that Action.

2. The Church that hath no Officers, may elect Officers or Ministers unto themselves. therefore it may also ordaine them; which Argument Dr. *Whitaker* useth as wee shall see anon. If it have Commission and power from Christ for the one, and that the greater, it hath it also for the other which is the lesser: Now ordination is lesse then election, and depends upon it as a necessary Antecedent by divine Institution, by vertue of which it is justly administred, being indeed nothing else but the admission of a person lawfully elected into his Office, or a putting of him into posssession thereof, whereunto he had right before by election, as was said before in answer to the precedent Question.

3. If a Church have Ministers or Elders before, then this ordination is to be performed by the Elders of the Church, and in their Assemblie, 1 *Tim.* 4. 14, as also many other acts are to be performed by them.

4. This

4. This Ordination thus performed by the Elders for the Church, may fitly be called the Act of the whole Church, as it is the whole man that seeth, that heareth, that speaketh, when these acts are instrumentally performed by the eye, the eare, and the tongue, in which sense Master *Parker* saith, *Ecclesia per alios docet, baptisatque, Polit. Eccles. l. 3. c. 7. p. 26.*

5. But when a Church hath no Officers, but the first Officers themselves are to be ordained, then this Ordination by the Rite of imposing of hands may be performed for the Church by the most prime, grave and able men from among themselves, as the Church shall depute hereunto, as the children of *Israel* did lay their hands upon the *Levites*, *Numb*. 8. 10. Now all the Congregation could not impose all their hands upon them together, all their hands could not possibly reach them together, and therefore it must needs be that some of the Congregation in the name of the whole body performed this Rite : And as this Scripture sheweth, that the people may in some cases lay their hands upon Church Officers, (for the *Levites* were such, upon whom the children of *Israel* did lay their hands) so let it be considered, whether these reasons doe not further make it manifest.

1. Men that are in no Office may elect, therefore they may ordaine, because ordination is nothing else but the execution of Election.

2. If it were not so, then one of these would follow, either that the Officers must minister without any Ordination at all, or else by vertue of some former Ordination received in some other Church, or else they must be ordained by some other Minister or Ministers of some other Church, that were ordained afore them, and so the Ministery to be by succession. But the first of these is against the Scripture, 1 *Tim*. 4. 14. *Heb*. 6. 2. And the second were to establish the Popish opinion of the indeleble Character, imprinted as they imagine in their Sacrament of holy Orders. Whereas for ought we can discerne, if when they are called to Office in any Church, they have need of a new Election, notwithstanding their former election into another Church

then,

then they have by the same ground need of a new Ordination, for Ordination depends upon Election: If their former Election be ceased, their former Ordination is ceased also; and they can no more minister by vertue of a former *Ordination* unto another *church*, then by vertue of a former Election. And for the third, we doe not understand what authority ordinary Officers can have to ordaine Ministers to such a Church, of which themselves are not so much as Members. Besides, at some times, namely at the first Reformation after the times of Popery, there were no others to be had but from the Pope, and his Bishops and Priests. Now it were a pittifull case, if the Sheep must have no Shepherd but such as are appointed to them by the wolves, That is, if Gods people might not have Ministers, but onely from the popish Bishops. This were to say, either that the Ministers of Antichrist, must, or may ordaine Ministers to the Church of Christ, or else that the popish Bishops are true Ministers of Christ. And if Protestants thinke it necessary, that their first Ministers should be ordained by the popish Bishops, it is no marvell if the Papists do thereupon beleeve that their Church is the true Church, and their Bishops true Ministers. Such a scandall is it unto them to maintaine this personall succession of the Ministery. But God doth so much abhorre *Antichrist*, that hee would not have his people to seek to him, nor his Priests to ordaine Chrifts Ministers, as he would not take [of *Babilon* a stone for a Corner, nor a stone for a foundation, *Ier.*51.26.

3. It is thus in civill Corporations and Cities, the Major, Bayliffe, or other chiefe Officer elect, is at his entrance and inauguration to receive at the hands of his Predecessors the Sword or Keyes of the City, or to have some other solemne Ceremonie by him performed unto him yet if either there be no former as at the first or that the former be dead or upon necessity absent, when his Successor entreth, then is this Ceremony and worke performed by some other, the fittest Instrument; neither need that City borrow any Officer of another City, neither could he entermeddle there without usurpation, though both the Corporations have the same Charter under the same King. And so it is in this

spiritual

spirituall Corporation or City, the Church of God.

4. That this point may seeme the lesse strange to you, we pray you consider with us a little further the nature of this Ordination, and then wee will adde the Testimonies of some eminent Protestant Writers in this case, that you may see this is not any singular opinion of ours. For the former, some indeed have so highly advanced this Ordination, that they have preferred it farre above preaching the Word, ministring the Sacraments, and Prayer, making it and the power of Excommunication, the two incommunicable Prerogatives of a Bishop above an ordianary Minister; yet the Scripture teacheth no such thing, but rather the contrary, for when the Apostles were sent out by Christ, there was no mention of Ordination in that Commission of theirs, but only of teaching & preaching & baptising *Mat.* 28. 19,20. *Mark.* 16. 15,16. If Ordination of Ministers had bin such a speciall worke, there would belike have bin some mention of it in their Commission. And certaine it is, the Apostles counted preaching the Word their principall worke, and after it Prayer, and the ministring of the Sacraments, *Act.* 6. 4. 1 *Cor.* 1. 17. If ordaining of Ministers had bin in their account so prime a worke, it may seem *Paul* would rather have tarried in *Creete* to have ordained Elders there, then have gone himselfe about preaching, leaving *Titus* for the other, *Tit.* 1 5. By all which it appeares, that ordaining of Ministers is not such an eminent work as that it is to be preferred above preaching the Word, and ministring the Sacraments, and therefore to be performed by them that are superiours unto ordinary Ministers; preaching and ministring the Sacraments, being left as inferiour workes unto Ministers, of an inferiour ranke, as they would have it, that stand for the superiority of Docesan Bishops; neither is it equall unto those other workes afore mentioned, that onely he that doth those, may performe this other also, as some others thinke; but being nothing else in the true nature and use of it but the execution and accomplishment and confirmation of election, it may bee performed by the people of God, that yet have no Officers, even as Election may upon which it doth depend.

5. Lastly,

5. Laſtly, let theſe ſayings of ſome Proteſtant Writers of
ſingular note, either for holineſſe, or learning, or both, be
well conſidered of. Maſter *Perkins* ſaith, Succeſsion of Doctrine alone is ſufficient ; for this Rule muſt bee remembred, that the power of the Keyes (that is, of order and ju-
riſdicticn) is tyed by God and annexed in the New Teſtament to Doctrine. If in *Turkey*, or *America*, or elſewhere,
the Goſpel ſhould be received by the counſell and perſwa-
ſion of private perſons, they need not ſend into *Europe* for
conſecrated Miniſters, but they have power to chooſe their
owne Miniſters from within themſelves ; becauſe where
God gives the Word he gives the power alſo ; *upon Gal* 1.11.
Doctor *Willet* ſaith, Whereas *Bellarmine* objecteth that as
in the old Law the Prieſthood went by earnall generation
and lineall deſcent from *Aaron*, ſo in the New it muſt bee
derived by ſucceſsion from the Apoſtles ; we anſwere, firſt,
that our Saviour Chriſt and his Apoſtles could ſhew no lineall deſcent from *Aaron*, neither had their ordination
from his Succeſſors, and yet were the true Paſtors of the
Church. And a little after, This we ſay further, that both
before Chriſt there were true Paſtors and Prophets, which
were not ordained by the Prieſts of *Aaron*; and ſince Chriſt,
that received not their ordination ſucceſsively from the
Apoſtles. Firſt, in the old Law, when the ordinary Prieſthood was corrupted, God raiſed up Prophets from other
Tribes that received not from the Prieſts their ordination
and allowance : ſuch an one was *Amos*, who was among
Heardſmen, and was made a Prophet as he was gathering
wilde black-berries. After the ſame manner in the corrupt
times of the Goſpel, the Lord hath raiſed up faithfull Miniſters to his Church, that could ſhew no ſucceſsion from
the degenerate Clergy. And a little after, If *Paul* were
made an Apoſtle without the ordination of the lawfull A-
poſtles much more may the Lord raiſe up new Paſtors to
his Church without ordination from the uſurpers of the
Apoſtles : *Synopſ. Papiſm. contr.* 2. *Q.* 3. *of Succeſsion Error* 20.
p. 81. *Morney* his words are full and plaine to the ſame purpoſe, *viz.* Although ſome of our men in ſuch a corrupt ſtate
of the Church, as we have ſeene in our time, without wait-

ing

ing for calling or allowance of them who under the title of
Paitors oppreiled the Lords Flock, did at firlt preach without this tormall calling, and afterward were chofen and
called to the holy Miniitey by the Churches which they
had taught ; yet this ought to feeme no more ftrange, then
if in a free common-wealth the people without waiting either for the eonfent, or for the voices of thofe that tyran-
nize over them, fhould (according to the Lawes) make
choice ot good and wife Magiftrates, fuch (happily) as
God would ferve his turne of for their deliverance, and for
the publike reftitution. And hereof wee have examples,
firlt, in the *Acts*, where wee read that *Philip*, who was but
a Deacon, preacheth in *Samaria* without the calling of the
Apoftles, yea without their privity, who for all that gave
their allowance to his worke. In *Frumentius*, carried upon
another occafion into the *Indies*, a meere Lay-man, who
yet there preacheth the Gofpel, and a good while after is
there made Bifhop. In thofe of whom *Origen* fpeaketh,
that fhall come by chance into a City where never any
Chriftian was borne, fhall there begin to teach, and labour
to inftruct the people in the Faith, whom the People fhall
afterward make their Paftors and Bifhops : and befides, in
all the Scriptures there is not one place that bindeth the
Miniftery of the Gofpel to a certaine fucceffion ; but con-
trariwife the Scripture fheweth, that God would fend two
fpeciail witnelfes to prophefie againft Antichrift : *Of the
Church chap.* 11.*p.*371. Doctor *Whitaker* anfwering *Bellarmine*, that would prove Proteftants to have no Church, becaufe their Minifters had no Ordination by Bifhops faith,
That as fometimes Bifhops were chofen by the Clergy and
fometimes by the People, fo the fame may be faid of Ordination, *viz.* that it was fometimes by the Clergy and fometimes by the People ; and then addeth, *Quid fi vocationem
eorum Episcoporum legitimam fuiffe concedat bellarminus, De ordinatione minus laboramus. Qui enim habent authoritatem vocan-
di, iidem etiam authoritatem ordinandi habent, fi legitima ordinatio non possit impetrari : nam ordinatio fequitur vocationem ; qui
vocatur, is quafi in fui muneris poffeffionem mittitur* : de Ecclef. Q.
5.cap.6 p.510. Finally, Doctor *Ames* doth alfo witnelfe
K the

the same in many places of his workes : for a taste take these few sayings of his in this case , *viz. Ad totam Ecclesiam semper pertinet ordinatio , quoad jus, vim , virtutem illam quam habet in Ministro Ecclesiæ constituendo ; sicut celebratio matrimonii vim aut virtutem omnem acceptam refert legitimo consensui conjugum : Ecclesiæ statu (ministerio & ordine deficiente) collapso vel corrupto, à plebe etiam actus iste ordinationis , quatenus necessarius est ad Ministri constitutionem in tali casu, potest legitimè exerceri,* Bellarm. enervat. lib. 3. de clericis , cap. 2 de ordinatione. And againe, a little after ; *Episcopos veros à veris Episcopis ordinarie dicimus ordinandos esse, sed nomine Ecclesiæ cui ordinantur.* And againe, a little after, *Potestas ordinandi est aliquo modo originaliter in tota Ecclesia, sicut potestas videndi originaliter est in toto animali, quamvis formaliter & subjectivè sit in oculo tantùm ; tum etiam ordinationis exercitium pendet à tota Ecclesia, sicut actus videndi hoc vel illud determinatè pendet non ab oculo sed à toto.* And againe, *Quamvis in Ecclesia benè constituta non debeat aliis quam presbyteris ordinandi manus mandari ; in defectu tamen idoneorum presbyterorum potest non presbyteris mandari.* And yet againe in the next place, *Si concedatur hoc, quòd ex ordine nemo possit esse legitimus pastor, nisi sit à legitimo Pastore & Episcopo ordinatus : In ordinis tamen defectu, cùm jam primò instaurari debet ordo, non potest tam accuratè observari, atque adeo extraordinarium aliquid tum potest intervenire sine ullo vitio.* These words you see are punctuall and plaine , that the power of ordaining Ministers is originally in the Church ; and that though when a Church hath Presbyters, the act of ordaining is to be done by those Presbyters ; yet in defect of such it may be performed by them that are no Presbyters, lawfully, and without fault ; which is the case of our Churches that are in their beginnings , and may be the case of any Church when they come to be without Officers, as by warre, pestilence, &c. it may come to passe.

T. 22.   There are some things common to Pastors with Teachers : as, that they are both Officers of the Church appointed by Christ ; both Elders or Bishops to rule and feed the Church, by labouring in the Word and Doctrine, *Act.* 20. 28 1 *Tim.* 3. 1. *Tit.* 1. 5, 7. and therefore the name of Pastour, in a generall sense may be given to them both , *Ier.* 3. 15.

3.15. as also the name of Teacher, *Isa.*30.20. as those names may also be given to Apostles, in as much as they also are Elders, Pastors, Teachers, to rule, to feed, to teach the Church of God,1*Pet.*5.1.*Ioh.*21.15.16. 1 *Tim.*2.7.& 2 1.11. And if Pastors and Teachers be both of them Church officers,to feed and rule the Church by labouring in the Word and Doctrine,they must not do this without application of it to the consciences and states of the hearers, as God shall helpe them : for this application is one part of his worke, that is by his office to preach the Word, without which the Word is not handled in such a manner as it ought to be, 2 *Tim.*2.15. 1 *Cor.*14.25. *Luk.*12.42. and many hearers need this, the Word delivered in generall without application of it being to them as bread set before children in the whole loafe. And if both of them must labour in the Word and Doctrine,and not onely in a generall way, but with application, we see not but they may both of them administer the Seales or Sacraments, wherein there is a speciall application of the promises of the Gospel, and the grace of Christ therein, unto the faithfull and believing receivers. 2. And yet for all this community betwcen them, they are not in propriety of speech the same Officers, but distinct, and so the Scripture speaketh of them *Ephes.*4.11. For if a man would say their Offices are confounded, because the same generall worke of preaching the Word, and applying the same, belongs unto them both : By the same reason a man might say the offices of Apostles and Evangelists were confounded ; for both of them were to preach the Word, with application of the same by doctrine, and Seales ; and also that the ordinary Pastors were the same office with them both, because hee also is to doe the same worke of preaching and applying : But an Apostle is to feed, and rule, and teach, by way of Doctrine and Application, as an Apostle ; an Evangelist as an Evangelist, and an ordinary Pastor as an ordinary Pastor, and therein lyes the difference : and wee may adde, a Teacher as a Teacher; and therein is he distinguished both from the Pastor, and from all other Church Officers, even as by the same they all are distinguished one from another, the same generall worke

of

of Doctrine and Application being common to them all.

3. And for the Teacher and Pastor, the difference between them lyes in this, that the one is principally to attend upon points of Knowledge and Doctrine, though not without Application; and the other to points of Practice, though not without Doctrine: and therefore the one of them is called, *He that teacheth*, and his worke is thus expressed, *let him attend on teaching* ; and the other, *He that exhorteth*, and his worke, *to attend on exhortation*, *Rom.*12.7,8. and the gift of the one is called *a word of knowledge*, and the gift of the other, *a word of wisedome*, 1 *Cor.*12.8. as experience also sheweth, that one mans gift is more doctrinall, and for points of knowledge; and anothers more exhortatory, and for points of practise.

To 23.   It is not the manner of Elders among us, whether Ruling onely, or Ruling and Teaching also, to strive for authority or preheminence one above another; as remembring what lesson our Saviour taught his Disciples, when they were at strife among them, which of them should be the greatest, *Luk.*22.24,25.&c. If *Diotrephes* strive for preheminence 3 *Ioh.*9,10. verily we abhorre such striving, and by the grace of God respect one another as Brethren. As for the peoples duty toward their Elders, it is taught them plainly in that place, 1 *Thes.* 5. 12, 13. as also in that of 1 *Tim.*5.17 *Let the Elders that rule well bee counted worthy of double honour, specially they that labour in the Word and Doctrine*; and this Word (*specially*) shewes them, that as they are to account all their *Elders worthy of double honour*, so in speciall manner their Teaching or Preaching Elders.

To 24.   These are answered in that which was sent the last
& 25. yeare.

To 26.   We doe believe that every Minister of the Gospel ought to be maintained with sufficient and honourable maintenance, according to his need and occasions, in regard of his person, calling charge of children and hospitality, so as he that preacheth the Gospel may in all these respects live
of

of the Gospel, 1 *Cor.*9.14. *Gal.*6.6. 1 *Tim.*5.17. And this
maintenance is not to be allowed as almes and courtesie,
but as debt and duty, to bee paid according to the rule of
Justice; the Labourer is worthy of his wages, *Luk.*10.17.
which the Apostle sheweth to be according to all Lawes of
nature, nations, *Moses* and Christ, 1 *Cor.*9. But for setled
and stinted maintenance, there is nothing done that way
amongst us, except from yeare to yeare, because the condi-
tions of Ministers may vary, and of the Church to which
they doe belong : Neither doe we know any such thing to
be appointed by Christ our Lord, for the maintenance of
the Ministery in these dayes ; but this we know that the
great mountaine burning with fire, cast into the sea upon
the sounding of the second Trumpet *Rev.*8.8,9. is applyed
by some good Writers to those times, when *Constantine*
brought setled endowments into the Church, with *ampla*
prædia (as they are called) are counted by some to bee no
better then poyson to the Church ; as the Stories say that
upon the fact of the good Emperour a voice was heard,
which said, *Hodie seminatum est virus in Ecclesiam.* And if
those Writers be not deceived which so expound that Scripture (as for our parts wee know not but they expound it
truely) then in as much as upon the casting of that mountaine into the sea, a third part of it became blood and a
third part of living creatures dyed, and a third part of ships
were destroyed, it may be truely gathered thence that the
bringing in of setled endowments and eminent preferments
into the Church, hath been the corruption, and to some
the destruction of such as lived by them, both Church-officers and Church-members.

We doe not permit, and call upon (such whom you call) *To* 27.
meere Lay men, and private persons, neither being in the
Ministery nor intended to it, ordinarily to preach or prophecy publiquely, in or before the Congregation, if by ordinarily, you meane frequently and usually. For where ordinary Officers are not wanting to a Church, and neither
detained from their worke by sicknesse, nor just absence, we
thinke it most meet to offer our Sacrifice to God and to the

Church

Church of our beſt gifts. But yet if you oppoſe ordinary to extraordinary, we doe confeſſe that ſome private members(to wit ſuch as are eminently fitted with knowledge and utterance, being alſo men of humble ſpirits, and holy lives, all which qualifications we finde but in a few) may without an extraordinary calling from God be called forth by by the Church upon ſome occaſion (and namely in the abſence or bodily weakneſſe of Miniſters, or for tryall of gifts when a man intends the Miniſtery) to ſpeake to edification, exhortation and comfort. *Iehoſaphat* ſent Princes (who neither were Miniſters nor intended ſo to be) to teach with the Prieſts and Levites, to wit, at leaſt to incourage the people, to hearken to the Prieſts and Levites come amongſt them, 2 *Chron.* 17. 7. 8. 9. As *Iehoſaphat* himſelfe alſo did the like, 2 *Chron.* 20. 20. Yea, and was their mouth alſo to God in prayer, *v.* 2. 5. to 13. As for that prophecying 1 *Cor.* 14. We conceive as ſome things in it be extraordinary, ſo ſome things ordinary. Extraordinary, that private men, and new converts ſhould be ſo ſoon & ſo ſuddainly, & ſo much enlightened & enlarged, as to be able to prophecy publikely to the edification of a whole Church: But yet this we conceive to be ordinary, that ſome private men may be found (at leaſt in ſome Churches) grown Chriſtians, of able gifts, who may have received a gift of Prophecy, and for ſuch we doe not thinke it requireth any more an extraordinary calling for them to prophecy in our Churches, then for *Iehoſaphat* and his Princes to prophecy in the Church of *Iſrael.*

To 28.   Our Anſwer to this Queſtion is that we never knew any Miniſters that did call upon the people thus to doe: and as for us, ſuch calling upon them is farre from us. All that we know to be holden in this caſe is this, that ſome thinke the people have a liberty to aske a Queſtion publiquely for their better ſatisfaction upon very urgent and weighty cauſe, though even this is doubted of by others, and all judge the ordinary practice of it, not neceſſary: but (if it be not meekly and wiſely carried) to be inconvenient if not utterly unlawfull, and therefore ſuch asking of Queſtions is ſeldome uſed in any Church among us, and in moſt Churches never. True it is in the times a little afore the Synod divers that were infected with corrupt opinions

were

were very bold,&forward in this kind of asking Queſtions, after *Sermons*,eſpecially when they had heard ſomthing delivered publiquely that did make againſt their Tenents; by which kind of asking Queſtions, they plainely diſcovered of what ſpirit they were, but for being called upon by us thus to doe, (as it ſeems to your Queſtion that you have been informed) the truth is,there was no ſuch matter.But now theſe men are long ſince (the greateſt part of them) to an Iſland(called *Aquedneck*)departed from amongſt us, ſome of them being excommunicated or baniſhed,or both, & others departing voluntarily, or for feare of the like cenſure, by meanes of which departure of theſe troubleſome ſpirits from amongſt us,and the bleſsing of God upon the Synod & Sermons that have laid open & reproved this diſorderly asking of Queſtions,a man may now live from one end of the year unto another in theſe Congregations, & not hear any man open his mouth in ſuch kind of asking Queſtions.

1. The converſion of ſinners unto God doth not alwaies *To* 29. follow the preaching of every one, that is in a lawfull office of miniſtery, as experience and Scripture doe aboundantly witneſſe, *Iſay.* 49. 4,5. & 53.1. *Ezech.* 3. 7. 2 *King.* 17.13 14. *Mat.* 11. 20 21. &c. *Iohn* 12. 37.

2. And when it doth follow, it is not by vertue of him, or of his office, but by vertue of Gods bleſsing, and the mighty operation of his ſpirit as he pleaſeth,without which the Miniſter and his office could have had no vertue at all to convert ſinners unto God, 1 *Cor.* 3.6. no more then *Peter* and *Iohn* could heale the lame man,by vertue of any power or holin ſſe that was in them, *Act.* 3. 12. For otherwiſe faithfull Miniſters ſhould not have their labours bleſſed for converſion ſome more and ſome leſſe. but all in the ſame meaſure inaſmuch as one of them is no more a Miniſter then another, nor no more in Office then another, their office being the ſame, the effect in converſion would bee the ſame if converſion were by the vertue of their office. The truth it is the Law of the Lord, (the whole Word of God that converts the ſoule, *Pſal.* 19. 7. And the Goſpell that is the power of God unto Salvation. *Rom.* 1. 16. And therefore the converſion of a man to God is to be aſcribed to God, and to the Word of his Grace: and not to the Miniſter,nor any vertue of his office. 3. But

3. But this we doe acknowledge, that the ſound converſion of ſinners, whenſoever ſuch a thing comes to paſſe, doth
argue that the Inſtruments of ſuch converſion are ſent of
God: God would not ſo have bleſſed them, as to convert
any by them, if himſelfe had not ſent them at all, *Rom.* 10.
14, 15. *Ier.* 23. 32.

4. And yet we dare not ſay, that Gods Word is not made
effectuall to converſion, unleſſe the man that ſpeakes it be a
Miniſter, that is to ſay, a Church Officer for the contrary
is evident from the Scripture, *John* 4 39. *Act.* 8. 4. with
11. 19, 20, 21. 1 *Cor.* 7. 16. They that were ſcattered abroad
upon the perſecution that aroſe about *Steven*, were not
Church Officers, at leaſt all of them (for the Apoſtles who
were their chiefe, if not their only preaching Officers, were
not ſcattered abroad upon that perſecution, but remained
ſtill at *Jeruſalem*, Acts 8. 1.) and yet theſe men did ſo preach
the Word of the Lord Jeſus to the *Iewes* and the *Grecians*,
that through the good hand of the Lord that was with
them, a great number believed and turned to the Lord; And
the ſame we ſay of the woman of *Samaria*, by whoſe Teſti-
monie of Chriſt many of the *Samaritans* believed on him.
To reſtraine the efficacy of Gods Word in ſuch ſort as to
ſay that none can be converted by it, unleſſe he that ſpeakes
it be a Miniſter, is to limit the ſpirit of the Lord, where he
hath not limited himſelf, who is free in working by whom
he pleaſeth, and as he will, 1 *Cor.* 12. 11. Even as the wind
bloweth where it liſteth, *Iohn* 3. 8. and ſometimes doth
bring to paſſe great things by weake meanes, that his owne
glory may be the more, 1 *Cor.* 1. 27, 28, 29. If any ſay, how
can theſe things ſtand together, that a man that is no Miniſter may be an Inſtrument of converſion, and yet converſion of ſinners argues that the man is ſent of God? Wee anſwer, that we muſt diſtinguiſh of ſending according to the
divers degrees thereof. For ſometimes it imports no more
but ſuch an Act of Gods diſpoſing providence, whereby
men are gifted and enabled for ſuch or ſuch a worke, and
permitted thereunto, though they have no command from
him for the doing thereof, nor doe it not with a ſincere
minde in any obedience to God, but for corrupt and ſiniſter
ends

ends of their owne. Thus God sent the King of *Assyria* against the *Iewes*, Isa. 10. 6. And bands of the *Caldees*, and bands of other Nations against *Jehojakim*, and against *Iudah*, to destroy it, 2 *King.* 24. 2. And yet they had no command from him to doe this, but sinned grievously in so doing. Thus they that preached Christ not sincerely, but of envie and strife, to adde affliction to *Pauls* bands, yet inasmuch as they preached Christ, might be said to be sent of God, and therefore the Apostle joyed at their preaching, *Phil.* 1. 15, 16. Thus *Baalam* in his Prophecies against the enemies of *Israel* and for the happy state of Gods people, might be said to be sent of God, though his heart and ends were corrupt and sinfull. But if men be not onely enabled with gifts for such or such a worke, but besides this, have a sincere minde and desire in the using thereof, to seeke the glory of God, and the good of soules, such men may much more be said to be sent of God, *Iohn* 7. 18. For these men have not onely abilities and gifts from God, and permission to imploy them as the former had, but also his spirit within them, which doth set their hearts on right and holy ends, which the other wanted. And yet if men doe want a lawfull office of Ministery, wherein to exercise those gifts or a lawfull calling to that office or exercise, they may in that respect be said not to be sent of God, or not to be called of him though sent of him, in the first or second respect. Thus in the Scriptures it is said of some they ran and I sent them not, *Ier.* 23. 21. I perceived that God had not sent him, but he pronounced his Prophecies, because *Sanballat* and *Tobiah* had hired him, *Neh.* 6. 12. And yet doubtlesse in respect of Gods disposing providence, he had sent them, as the Scripture witnesseth, that God sends strong delusions and lying Prophets, and unfaithfull Shepherds, 2 *Thes.* 2. 11. 1 *King.* 22. 22, 23. *Zech.* 11. 16. to be a plague unto the Sons of men, and for tryall to his servants, *Deut.* 13. 3. 1 *Cor.* 11. 19. Now let these distinctions be applyed to the case in hand, and we may perceive how, if a man convert sinners, certainly God sends him; and yet some that are not called to any office in the Ministery, may through his blessing convert sinners : A man converts none unlesse God send him in the first or second sence, and yet he may convert, and not bee sent, if sending be taken in the third sence, that is for a lawfull calling into some office in the

L Church.

Church. And wee may adde, further a man may be sent in this third sence and yet convert none if he be not also sent in the first an second respect; that is, a man may have a lawfull calling outwardly unto a lawfull office in the Church, and yet not convert sinners, if he want gifts or sincerity of heart, which might be the case of *Iudas*, and of many wicked Priests in the old Testament: Yea, happily convert none though he be truly sent in all three respects, as was said before in the beginning of the Answer to this Quære. But if comparison be made, we doubt not, but whilest the Ministery remaines uncorrupt, God is wont to follow with a greater blessing the labours of those who have gifts and an office of Ministery also, then of those who have gifts alone without office. He is willing, and wonted to honour himselfe most, where most of his wayes are observed.

To 30.   Master *Parker Polit. Ecclef. l. 2. c. 39. & c. 41.* observes a difference between the Substantialls in Church Politie, and the accessaries or accidentalls, and circumstantialls: And againe, that of circumstances some are generall, and some particular and individuall; and so sheweth that the Church Politie in regard of the substantialls thereof is prescribed in the Word, and therefore immutable. According to which distinction wee Answer, that if those words (precisely the same course) mentioned in this Question, be not meant of particular and individuall circumstances, but only of the substantialls or generall circumstances, then for ought we know there is no materiall point, either in constitution, or government, wherein the Churches in *N. E.* (viz. In the bay, in the jurisdiction of *Plymouth*, at *Connectacute*, and *Quilipiake*) do not observe the same course.(And sure it is, if they doe not they ought, because Christ hath left but one way for all Churches, and the same to be observed to the Worlds end, *1 Tim. 6. 13,14.*) Onely, that conformity to the Lyturgie and Ceremonies in some places, to the Northward, that Anabaptisme at *Providence*, and Familisme at *Aquidneck* hinders that we cannot say the same of them, nor of any other in *N. E.* that concurre with them in their unwarrantable wayes, if there be any such, though thankes be to God there is none within this Jurisdiction.

To 31.   Who must have liberty to sit downe in this Common-wealth and enjoy the liberties thereof is not our place to determine, but
the

the Magiſtrates who are the rulers and governours of the Common-wealth, and of all perſons within the ſame. And as for acknowledging a company to be a ſiſter Church, that ſhall ſet up, and practiſe another forme of Church Diſcipline, being otherwiſe in ſome meaſure, as you ſay, approveable, we conceive the companie that ſhall ſo doe, ſhall not be approveable therein. For the Diſcipline appointed by Jeſus Chriſt for his Churches is not arbitrary, that one Church may ſet up and practice one forme, and another another forme as each one ſhall pleaſe, but is one and the ſame for all Churches, and in all the Eſſentialls and Subſtantialls of it unchangable, and to be kept, till the appearing of Jeſus Chriſt, 1 *im.* 6. 13,14. from which place Maſter *Cartwright* obſerves the perpetuity of Church Government taught by the Apoſtles, unto the end of the World, and is plain and large in this point, 1 *Rep. p.* 177. as is likewiſe Mr. *Parker Polit. Ecclef. l. 2. c.* 42. and ſo forward to the end of that Book, unto whom we refer you herein. And if that Diſcipline which we here practiſe, be (as we are perſwaded of it) the ſame which Chriſt hath appointed and therefore unalterable, we ſee not how another can be lawfull; and therefore if a company of people ſhall come hither and here ſet up and practiſe another, we pray you thinke not much, if we cannot promiſe to approve of them in ſo doing, eſpecially untill wee ſee how approvable the men may be, and what Diſcipline it is that they would ſet up. For ſhould wee in ſuch generall words as is there expreſſed, promiſe to accept of a companie as a Siſter Church, that ſhall ſet up and practiſe another Diſcipline, and then ſhould be taken at the utmoſt extent of our words, we might by this meanes be bound to accept of a company of Papiſts, or Arminians, or Familiſts, or Anabaptiſts, as a ſiſter Church, for there is none of theſe but ſomething may be found in them, and in their Diſcipline, that is in ſome meaſure approveable. And yet we pray you heartily in the Lord, ſo conceive of us in this paſſage, that we are farre from making any ſuch compariſon,as if your ſelves were not approved in our conſciences far above the beſt of ſuch men, yea and above our ſelves in many reſpects.

We have ſaid before in that which we ſent you the laſt yeare, and upon this occaſion we ſay it now againe, that you are in our hearts (if the Lord would ſuffer) to live and dye together: and therefore if this Queſtion were meant of your ſelves, or any of you, and a company of godly people joyning with you (as it may be it is, though we cannot certainly ſay it, becauſe you doe not expreſſe ſo much) we thinke if you were here, wee ſhould gladly accept of you and your people as a ſiſter-Church, and that you would doe the like to ours; and yet not when you ſhould ſet up and practiſe one forme of Church-diſcipline, and we another; but becauſe we are perſwaded if you were here, you would ſet up and practiſe the very ſame that wee doe, and not any other: or elſe if we be ſwerving from the rule in any particular (as God knowes we are but weake men, and far from dreaming of perfection in this life) God would by you ſend in more light unto us then yet we ſee, and make you inſtruments in his hand for perfecting what is here begun according to his will, for ſtrengthening what is weake, and reforming what may be found to be amiſſe: For we truſt in the Lord, that as wee are deſirous that you might joyne with us in the wayes wherein we now walke, (which we doe not ſee but they are according to the Rule) ſo we ſhould be as willing to receive light from you, and to redreſſe (as God ſhall helpe us) whatſoever by you or any other he may diſcover to us to ſtand in need of Reformation. For which cauſe among others we doe the more earneſtly deſire, if it were the Lords will that he might ſend you hither, nothing doubting but if you were here, there would be ſuch agreement between you and us, that either you would approve of the things which we beleeve and practiſe, or that we ſhould approve of what you may ſhevv us to be more agreeable to the minde of Chriſt: and then there would be no occaſion of ſuch a Queſtion, *Whether we may ſet up and practiſe another diſcipline, and yet be accepted as a ſiſter-Church:* but rather of bleſsing the Lord, when that ſhall be accompliſhed in you and us which is written in the Prophets, *I will give them one heart and one way: I will turne unto the people a pure language, that they may all call upon the Name of the Lord, to ſerve him with one conſent,* Jer.32.39. Zeph.3.9. *Wee have confidence in you through the Lord, that you will be none otherwiſe minded; but if in any thing ye be otherwiſe minded God ſhall reveale even this unto you,* Gal.5.10. Phil.3.15.

To 32.   This was anſwered in the anſwer to Poſit.1.& 2.ſent unto you the laſt yeare.

F I N I S.

AN
APOLOGIE

OF THE CHVRCHES
IN *NEW-ENGLAND*
FOR *CHVRCH-COVENANT*.

OR,

A Difcourfe touching the Covenant
between God and men, and efpecially concerning *Church-Covenant*, that is to fay, The
Covenant which a Company doe enter into when
they become a Church; and which a parti-
cular perfon enters into when he be-
comes a member of a Church.

Sent over in Anfwer to Mafter BERNARD,
in the Yeare 1 6 3 9.
And now publifhed for the fatisfaction
of all who defire refolution in this point.

LONDON,
Printed by *T. P.* and *M. S.* for *Beniamin Allen.*
1 6 4 3.

A DISCOVRSE TOVCHING THE

Covenant between *God* and *Men*,
and especially concerning *Church-
Covenant*, that is to say, the *Covenant* which a Company do enter into
when they become a Church, and
*which a particular perfon enters
into when he becomes a member of a Church.* 1639.

JER. 50. 5.

*Come let us joyne our felves to the Lord, in a perpetuall
Covenant that fhall not be forgotten.*

Lthough that which is foretold in thefe two Chap-
ters, and namely in the fourth and fifth verfes of
this Chapter, was in part fulfilled when the people
of God returned from Captivitie in *Babylon* at the
end of feventie yeares : yet we muft not limit the
place to that time onely, but may extend it further
to the dayes of the Gofpel, and the fpirituall return, not of the Jews
onely, but of the Gentiles alfo, when men fhall be converted from
Pagan, Antichriftian, Babylonifh, or Jewifh bondage and captivitie, or from flavery to finne, and felf-righteoufneffe, and fhall be
joyned to God in the fellowfhip of his Church, in the dayes of the
New Teftament. For as fome paffages in this Scripture were never fully accomplifhed at the returne from the captivitie of the feventie yeares, and namely this, that the children of *Ifrael* and *Judah* fhould returne both together : (for the ten tribes returned not

A   at at all :) so many things that literally concerned the Jewes were types and figures, signifying the like things concerning the people of God in these latter dayes : In which respect sincere converts are called Jewes, *Rom.* 2. 29. and Israelites, *Gal. 6. 16. Joh.* 1. 47. and our Sacraments are made Antitypes of theirs, 1 *Cor.* 10. 1, 2, 3. and Rome is called Babylon, *Rev.* 17. 5. and Papists are called Gentiles, *Rev.* 11. 2. and therefore the captivitie of Babylon might well be a Type of the spirituall captivitie of Gods people to Antichristian bondage, and their returne from Babylon to Sion, a type of the returne of Christians from Romish slavery to the true Sion, the Christian Church. And this may be added further, that this place seemes not onely to be meant of the private or personall conversion of this or that particular Christian, but also further, of the open and joynt calling of a company, because it is said, they shall come, the children of *Israel* and the children of *Judah* together, and that their saying shall not be, *Let me joyne, &c.* but in the Plurall number, *Let us joyne our selves unto the Lord,* so noting the joyning of a company together in holy Covenant with God.

   Concerning which Covenant with God, it will not be amisse for the better understanding of that which followes ; first, briefly to shew how diversly Covenant is taken in the Scripture, which sometimes imports generally any firme appointment or promise of God, when m .doth not promise unto God any thing backe againe : Thus the preserving of *Noah* in the Arke, and of the world from being drowned any more by a floud ; the interchangeable succession of day and night ; the giving of the Priesthood unto *Phineas* ; the setting forth of the Shew-bread every Sabbath before the Lord, and the giving of the heave-offering unto the Priests, are said to be done by a Covenant, or an everlasting Covenant of God, *Gen.* 6. 18 & 9. 9, 10, 11. *Jer.* 33. 20. *Num.* 25. 12, 13. *Levit.* 24. 8. *Num.* 18. 19.. But sometimes Covenant is taken more strictly and properly, for an agreement which God doth make with men, when he promiseth some blessing unto men, and bindes them to performe some dutie backe againe to him. Taken thus it hath two parts : first, a promise or stipulation of some blessing on Gods part : secondly, Restipulation or promise, or binding of man unto dutie back againe on his part : both these are in those words of the Covenant, *I will be to thee a God, thou shalt be to me a people :* and so *Gen.* 17. 1, & v. 7, 8 9, 10. The Co-

venant

venant taken thus is either the Covenant of workes, or the Covenant of grace : And againe the Covenant may be considered, first as it is personall, private and particular, between God and one particular soule, making Covenant with God, and God with him, either at his first conversion, or at other times; of which we reade 2 *Sam.* 23. 5. & *Psal.* 119. 106. & 66. 13,14. & 27. 8. & *Psal.* 119. 7, 8 Secondly, it is generall and publick of a company joyntly together, of which this Text *Jer.* 50. 5. seemes most properly to speake : as also that *Deut.* 29. 9, 10, &c. and that *Exod.* 19. 5, 6, and many others : A Covenant taken thus generally when it respects spirituall blessings, and spirituall duties, in the Communion of Saints, is that which is called Church-covenant, which Church-Covenant differs not in substance of the things promised from that which is between the Lord and every particular soule, but onely in some other respects; as first, the one is of one Christian in particular, the other of a company joyntly together. Secondly, if right Order be observed, a man ought not to enter into Church-Covenant, till he be in Covenant with God before, in respect of his personall estate. Thirdly, The one is usually done in private, as in a mans Closet between the Lord and his soule, and the other in some publick assembly. Fourthly, The one in these dayes is of such duties as the Gospel requires of every Christian as a Christian, the other of such duties as the Gospel requires of every Church and the members thereof.

Now concerning Church-Covenant, two things are to be noted for the better understanding thereof : first, the description of it : secondly, the use of it, and the benefit and fruit thereof. For " the former it may be thus described, *viz. A solemne and publick* " *promise before the Lord, whereby a company of Christians, called by the* " *power and mercy of God to fellowship with Christ, and by his providence* " *to live together, and by his grace to cleave together in the unitie of faith,* " *and brotherly love, and desirous to partake together in all the holy Ordi-* " *nances of God, doe in confidence of his gracious acceptance in Christ,* " *binde themselves to the Lord. and one to another, to walke together by* " *the assistance of his Spirit, in all such wayes of holy worship in him, and* " *of edification one towards another, as the Gospel of Christ requireth of* " *every Christian Church, and the members thereof.*

In this description, there are comprised six things : First, the generall name of the thing : [*a solemne and publick promise*] a pro-

mise

mife it is, and therefore it is called, a joyning in Covenant here: an entring into Covenant, *Deut.* 29. 10. Solemne and publick, and therefore it is by the children of *Israel* and the children of *Judah* together : and they fay, *let us joyne.* Secondly , The object [*the Lord, and one another*] *joyne our felves to the Lord.* it is not a promife onely to man, but to the Lord himfelfe, and likewife to one another; for, *come let us joyne,* implyes mutuall confent together. Thirdly, The Agents or the qualification of the perfons : [*Chriftians*] not Turkes, Indians, &c. Saints, *Pfal.* 50. 5. 16, 17. [*called to fellowfhip with Chrift*] fo 1 *Cor.* 1. 9 elfe if they be not united to Chrift by faith, they are not fit materialls for fuch a building as a Church of God, which is the houfe of the living God, *Ephef.* 1. 1. 1 *Cor.* 1. 2. *Phil.* 1. 1. *Rev.* 21. 27. [*By his providence to live together*] elfe they cannot partake in the Lords Ordinances together as Churches ought to doe, 1 *Cor.* 14. 23. *Act.* 14. 27. the whole Church comes together in one place [*cleaving together in faith and love*] fo *Act.* 4. 32. If they differ, namely, in opinion, or in their affection, and fhould joyne in this Covenant, breaches, factions, rents, and fchifmes, would be like to be the iffue of fuch joyning : things fo unlike would not clofe nor long hold together, *Dan.* 2. 43 [*Defirous to partake in all Ordinances*] this fhould be the ground of their joyning in Covenant together, *Pfal.* 110. 3. willing : and not pride, nor gaine, nor the like : Fourthly, The Act [*binde themfelves*] that now they are bound by their owne word and promife, that they may fay now, as *Pfal.* 56. 12. *Thy vowes are upon me*, or as *Num.* 30. 2. if he binde his foule with a vow. Fiftly, The matter promifed ; [*To walke together in all fuch wayes of worfhip and mutuall edification, as the Gofpel requireth of Churches and Church-members*] they binde not themfelves to obferve any devifes of their owne, nor inventions of men, but fuch things as the word of God requireth ; neither is it perfect obedience to the Law, for that were impoffible to performe, and prefumption to promife; nor is it onely in generall the duties of the Gofpel, but fpecially fuch duties of worfhip to God, &edification of one another as concerne Church-State, which now they enter into. Sixtly, The manner of performing [*Confidence of Gods gracious acceptance and affiftance through Chrift*] for in all our wayes God muft be acknowledged, *Pro.* 3. 6. and much more in fuch fpeciall matters of weight : If men in entring into this Covenant looke for acceptance, through any worth

of

of their owne, or promife dutie in their own ftrength, they fhew themfelves like to the Pharifees, *Luk.* 18.10, 11. and turne the Church-Covenant into a Covenant of workes: and as many as are of the workes of the Law, are under the curfe, *Gal.* 3. 10.

The ufe and benefit of this Church-Covenant, and the fruit thereof, may be feene in two particulars; firft, That this is that whereby a company of Chriftians doe become a Church : It is the Conftituting forme of a Church. Secondly, This is that by taking hold whereof a particular perfon becomes a member of a Church, which was conftituted afore. For the former of thefe ; every Chriftian Church muft have in it both matter and forme, and as the matter by Gods appointment are vifible Saints, or vifible beleevers, *Ephef.* 1. 1. 1 *Cor.* 1. 2. and in the New Teftament, onely fo many as may meete together in one Congregation : So the forme is a uniting, or combining, or knitting of thofe Saints together into one vifible body, by the band of this holy Covenant. Some union or band there muft be amongft them, whereby they come to ftand in a new relation to God, and one towards another, other then they were in before : or els they are not yet a Church, though they be fit materialls for a Church ; even as foule and body are not a man, unleffe they be united ; nor ftones and timber an houfe, till they be compacted and conjoyned.

Now that a company becomes a Church, by joyning in Covenant, may be made good fundry wayes ; firft, By plaine Texts of Scripture ; as from *Deut.* 29. 1, 10, 11, 12, 13. *Yee ftand this day all you before the Lord your God, your Captaines of your Tribes, your Elders, your Officers, with all the men of Ifrael,* ver. 10. *That thou shouldeft enter into Covenant with the Lord thy God,* ver. 12. *and he may eftablish thee for a people unto him'elfe,* ver. 13. So that here is plainly shewed, that here was a company, *ver.* 10. and this company were to be eftablished to be a people unto the Lord, that is to fay, a Church, *ver.* 13. And this is done by the peoples entring into folemne Covenant with God, *ver.* 12. And therefore a company of people doe become a Church by entring into Covenant with God.

"*This Covenant was not like our Church-Covenants, for it was of all* *Object.* 1 "*the Nation together; whereas the Church-Covenant with us, is of fome* "*feleɛt perfons, leaving out others.*

1. This Objection concerns the matter of a Church, but the *Anfwer.* Covenant is not the materiall caufe of a Church, but the formall

caufe

A 3

cause thereof: and for this the Text is plaine and expresse, that by entring into Covenant with God, a people come to be the Lords people, that is to say, his Church.

2. If it was of all the people together, the reason was because that Church was a nationall Church : now if a nationall Church becomes a Church by entring into solemne Covenant with God, then a Congregationall Church becomes a Church by the same means ; for there is no difference between them in this point.

3. Though it was of all the people, we may not say it proves that when we looke at the materiall cause of a Church, there may be a promiscuous taking in of all Commers without distinction or separation of the precious from the vile ; for, first, when God took in this Nation to be his people, he separated them from all the Nations of the earth besides : so that there was a distinction and separation of some from others. Secondly, this generation was generally a generation of beleevers ; for it was they that were to enter into the land within a while after; for they were fortie yeares in the Wildernesse. & this Covenant was made in the last moneth save one of the last of those fortie yeares, *Deut.*1.3. And their carkasses fell not in the Wildernesse through unbeliefe, as their Fathers did, *Num* 14.*Heb.*3. but entred by faith, and when they were entred, subdued Kingdomes by their faith, *Heb.*11.33. and served the Lord all the dayes of *Joshua*, and of the Elders that outlived *Joshua*, Josh. 24.31. As for that which is said of them, *ver.*4,5. of this Chap. that the Lord had not given them eyes to see, &c. that proves not that they were wholly hardned in a carnall estate, but onely that they were dull and slow of heart to consider of sundry dispensations of God towards them; for as much is said of the disciples of Christ, *Mar.*8.17,18. when doubtlesse they were not meere carnall or naturall persons.

Object. 2   "*This people* Deut. 29. *could not become the Lords people by entring* "*into solemne Covenant with God, for they were the Lords Church and people already before this.*

Answer.   1. If they were, yet that was by entring into solemne Covenant with God on Mount *Sinai*, when the Lord had brought them up out of the Land of *Ægypt* ; for then they entred into solemne Covenant with God, and God with them, and so they became the Lords peculiar people, *Exod.* 19 4,5,6,8.&c. If they were his people before that, yet that also was by Covenant made with them in the

the loynes of *Abraham*, when God tooke him and his seede to be his Church and people, yet separating *Ishmael* from *Isaac* and *Esau* from *Jacob*, that the inheritance of the Covenant of God, and of being the Church of God, might rest in the house of *Jacob*.

2. Yet it was not without great reason that the Lord should now establish them by solemne Covenant to be a people to him-selfe, because the Nation had been much degenerated from the spirit and wayes of *Abraham* in *Ægypt*, and had broken that Cove-nant by their Idolatries there, *Ezek.* 20. 7, 8. And the Covenant made in *Sinai* or *Horeb* when they were come out of *Ægypt*, they had also broken by their Idolatries in the Wildernesse, *Ezek.* 20. 13, 16. for which causes, and the like, the Lord consumed that generation, that they never entred into the Land, *Josh.* 5. 4, 6. And therefore now when their posteritie and children were ready to enter in, the Lord entred into Covenant with them, and there-by established them to be his people, their Fathers being cut off for breaking the Covenant. But still it was by Covenant that both Fathers first, and children afterward became a Church and people unto God ; and when this generation were entred into the Land, their Covenant made before between God and them, was confir-med by Circumcision, *Josh.* 5. 3. 7. they being not Circumcised before.

" But this Covenant was of the whole Church with God, and therefore **Object.3** " not like our Church-Covenants, which are between the Church and the " members, concerning watchfulnesse over one another, and the like.

Our Church-Covenants are with the Lord himselfe, as was **Answer.** shewed before in the description thereof. For watchfulnesse and duties of edification one towards another, are but branches of the Lords Covenant, being duties commanded by the Law : and so it was with that people of *Israel*, who when they promised and Co-venanted to walke in all the wayes of God ; in all his statutes and commandements and judgements, they promised these duties of love and watchfulnesse and edification one towards another, be-cause these were duties commanded and required of God, *Lev.* 19. 17. *Deut.* 29. 18. the neglect whereof in the matter of *Achan* was the sinne of all the Congregation, and brought judgement upon them all, *Josh.* 7. 11, 12. Yea by this Covenant they were bound to duties towards them that were not then present, but children af-terward to be borne, and proselytes, that afterward should be added

ded to them, *ver.* 14, 15. Like as our Church-Covenants are with
them that now are, and that hereafter shall become members of
the same Church. When *Jehojada* made a Covenant between the
King and the people, 2 *King.* 11. 17. that Covenant was but a
branch of the Lords Covenant with them all, both King and people: for the King promised but to Rule the people righteously, according to the will of God : and the people to be subject to the
King so Ruling. Now these duties of the King to them , and of
them to the King, were such as God required in his Covenant,
both of him and them : and so it is in Church-Covenant,the duties
of the Church to the members, and the members to the Church,
and one another, are no other but such as the Gospel and the Covenant of grace requireth both of the Church and the members of
it in their severall places.

Object.4   "But this place of Deut. 29. is not sufficient to prove a Church-Cove-
"nant in these dayes : because it is in the Scriptures of the old Testament,
"for whatsoever must be used in the dayes of the New Testament,must be
"proved from the Scriptures of the New Testament, or else it is to be
"layd aside.

Answer.   1. The Church Covenant may be proved from the New Testament also as will afterwards appeare.

2. But suppose there were not pregnant places for it in the New
Testament, yet it is not enough to prove the same unlawfull : for
whatsoever Ordinance of the old Testament is not repealed in the
New Testament, as peculiar to the Jewish Pædagogie, but was of
morall and perpetuall equitie, the same bindes us in these dayes,
and is to be accounted the revealed will of God in all ages, though
it be not particularly and expressely mentioned in the writings of
the New Testament, else how shall we prove it unlawfull for a
man to marry his Sister,or his Aunt ? How shall we prove it warrantable and necessary for Magistrates to punish Sabbath-break-
ing,blasphemy, and Idolatry ? How shall we prove it lawfull to
apply the seale of Gods Covenant unto Infants? or to admit women to eate of the holy things ; for the Scriptures of the New Testament doe speake little in these cases ; onely the Scriptures of the
Old Testament doe give direction, and light about them,*Lev.*18.
& 19. *Neh.* 13.15. &c. 2 *Chron.* 15. 16. & 2 *King.* 23. *Gen.* 17. 2.
& *Exod.* 12. 4. 6. And the New Testament hath nothing to the
contrary, and they are all according to morall equitie and reason,
                                                            and

and therefore they are to be obferved from the Scriptures of the Old Teftament, as the revealed will of God, though there were nothing expreffely for them in the New. And the fame we fay of the particular in hand. For, that a company fhould be combined together into one body, in way of Government and fubjection, by way of mutuall free Covenant; as men doe when they enter into Church Eftate, nothing is more naturall or agreeable to morall equitie; nay, it implyeth a contradiction in the very name of libertie or freedome, that free-men fhould take upon them authoritie or power over free men without their free confent, and voluntary and mutuall Covenant or Engagement. And therefore feeing this Covenant is not repealed in the Scriptures of the New Teftament, the Scriptures of the Old are fufficient warrant for it.

Another Scripture to prove the fame, is *Deut.* 26. 16, 17, 18. with *Deut.* 27. 9. *This day the Lord hath commanded thee to doe thefe Statutes and Judgements, thou fhalt therefore keepe and doe them, &c. Thou haft avouched the Lord this day to be thy God, and to walke in his wayes, and to keepe his Statutes, &c. And the Lord hath avouched thee this day to be his peculiar people; Take heed and hearken, O Ifrael, this day thou art become the people of the Lord thy God.* This Scripture plainly fhewes thefe things: 1. That here was the making of a Covenant between God and man; for that avouching of God to them, and them to God, was the making of Covenant, *ver.* 17 18. 2. This was not of one perfon, but of a company together, the whole people of *Ifrael,* 26. 18. & 27. 9. 3 Here is the effect of this Covenant, that thereby they become the Lords people, *ver.* 9. So that when a company doe enter into holy Covenant with God, they become thereby the Lords people, that is to fay, his Church. So *Ezech.* 16. 8. proves the fame likewife: *I entred into Covenant with thee, faith the Lord, and thou becam'ft mine.* Here alfo is the making of Covenant between the Lord and men; and this Covenant was not perfonall, but of a company; for it was with Hierufalem, *ver.* 2. which was a whole Citie; it was with them that were multiplied as the bud of the feild, *ver.* 7 and it was with them that did profper into a kingdome, *ver.* 13. and therefore not meant onely of any one particular perfon: And by this Covenant they became the Lords; that is, the Lords Church and people; for it is exprefly faid, *I entred into Covenant with thee, and thou becameft mine.* So that when a company enter into Covenant with God, and God with

B   them,

them, they become thereby the Lords Church and people. Likewife *Ezek.* 20. 37. *I will caufe you to paffe under the rod; and I will bring you into the bond of the Covenant.* In which place, there is firft mention of an holy Covenant. Secondly, This was not of one perfon, but of a company, the whole houfe of Ifrael, *ver.* 30. 39. Thirdly, And this Covenant is called a *Bond,* becaufe it is by Covenant that a people are bound, and tyed, and knit together, as one Church, all of them unto the Lord, and one unto another, So that the Covenant is the bond of union, by which a company are fo combined and united, as that they become a Church It is alfo obfervable, how the Lord before he would bring them into this bond of the Covenant, he would *caufe them to paffe under the rod*; by which phrafe, as *Junius* upon the place well obferves, is meant tryall and probation; drawne from the manner of Shepheards or owners of Cattell, who went among their fheepe, or other cattell with a rod, and therewith pointed out fuch as were for the Lords holy ufe, as *Lev.* 27. 32. And fo hereby is noted that God would not in the dayes of the Gofpel have men to be brought into his Church hand over head, but he would firft caufe them to paffe under the rod of due tryall and probation; and then fuch as upon tryall were found to be holy for God, or meete matter for his Church, fhould folemnly enter into Covenant with God, and that Covenant fhould be the bond that fhould combine them, and knit them together into one, that fo they that were many particular perfons, fhould all become one body, that is to fay, a Church.

And fo much of the firft Argument drawne from plaine Texts of Scripture.

Argu. 2.   A fecond Argument may be taken from the Titles that are given to the Church; as firft, that the Church is faid to be married or efpoufed unto Chrift, *Jer.* 2. 2. *&* 3. 14. 2 *Cor.* 11. 2. From whence the Argument may be formed thus : If every Church becomes a Church by being married or efpoufed unto Chrift, then a company becomes a Church by way of Covenant: But the former is true, therefore the latter is true alfo.

The Affumption, that a Church becomes a Church by being married unto Chrift, is plaine from the former Scriptures, where the   hutch of *Ifrael,* and the Church of *Corinth,* in regard of their entring into Church Eftate, are faid to be efpoufed and married unto Chrift, as a loving and chaft Virgine to one husband. Which
                                                                    fpirituall

spirituall marriage between Christ and his Church, is also taught in the type of the marriage between King *Salomon* and *Pharoahs* daughter, *Psal.* 45.

The Consequence of the Proposition is plaine in reason; for there is no marriage but by way of Covenant;no woman becomes a mans wife, but by way of bestowing her selfe in Covenant upon such a man: neither doth a man become an husband, but by the same means; and therefore the Scripture speaking of the violation of marriage, calls it a violation of Covenant, *Prov.* 2. 17.

" *Christ hath but one wife or Spouse,* Cant. 6 9. *Object.* 1.

Answer.
The Catholique Church indeed is but one; *viz.* the whole company of Gods Elect in heaven, in earth, dead, now living, and not yet borne: But as there is the Church - Catholique, which is but one; so there are particular and visible Churches, which are in number many; and therefore the Scripture speakes of Churches, 2 *Cor.* 8. 1. 19. *Gal.* 1. 2. Of the Churches of the Gentiles, *Rom.* 16. 4. Of seven Churches, *Rev.* 1. 4. Of all Churches, 1 *Cor.* 14 33. & 7 17. *Rev.* 2. 23.

" *But if every particular Church be the Wife of Christ, how many hun-* *Obj.* 2.
" *dred Wives should he have?*

Answ.
1. If the Church of Israel, *Jer.* 2 2. the Church of *Corinth,* 2 *Cor.* 11. 2. The Jewish Church, *Rev.* 19. 7. be the Spouse and wife of Christ, there is no reason but others should be the same also, especially seeing there is no particular Church, but in respect of their Church estate, they may decline and goe a whoring from Christ, and that shews that they were first espoused to him; for no woman can be said to goe a whoring from a man, if shee were never married, nor espoused to him at all.

2. This that seemes an absurditie, and were a sinfull practise among men, in respect of Christ, is a certaine truth, and no dishonour unto him at all, to have more Spouses then one upon earth, many spirituall Spouses. Men cannot give themselves wholly and intirely to many as Christ can. Every faithfull soule is espoused and married unto Christ; and in that respect he hath not onely many hundred but many thousand, yea many millions of spirituall Spouses.

" *But this spirituall marriage is between Christ and the Church, But* *Obj*
" *the Church-Covenant is between the Church and the members, and*
" *therefore this marriage doth not prove the Church-Covenant.*

1. In

Answer.   1. In some sort there may be said to be a marriage between the Church and the members, *viz.* in respect of that deare love and affection, that ought to be between them ; and therefore it is said, *As a young man marrieth a Virgine, so shall the children of the Church be married to the Church,* Isa. 62. 5.

2. But properly the marriage is between Christ & the Church, and so is the Covenant also, so farre as therein they give up themselves to Christ as unto an head and Lord ; as a woman in the Covenant of marriage doth give up her selfe unto her husband ; And the performance of such duties as the Church and the member owe one unto another, is a branch of that marriage-Covenant, wherein they are tyed to Christ ; for Christ himselfe in his Covenant requires, not onely that they should give up themselves to him, but also that they should performe these duties one unto another. And accordingly it is said of the Churches in *Macedonia,* that *they gave up themselves first to the Lord, and then to us by the will of God,* 2 Cor. 8. 5. True it is, they doe also binde themselves by Covenant one unto another, but in that respect the Covenant is properly a brotherly Covenant ; like that 1 *Sam.* 20. 8. *Amos* 1. 9. because there the engagement is to one another as brethren, fellow-members, and fellow-helpers, and not as to one head or Lord, as it is in respect of Christ, and therefore in that respect it is not so properly a marriage-Covenant as it is in respect of Christ : though duties to one another are promised in their Covenant with one another, and also in their Covenant with Christ. In briefe thus : They promise unto Christ duties to him, and duties to one another according to him : and so their Covenant is a marriage-Covenant with Christ : They promise also to one another, duties to one another, and so it is a brotherly Covenant.

Another Title given to the Church (which also proves that a Church is made by Covenant) is the Title of a Citie, or Citie of God, *Psal.* 87 3. & 48 1. 8. & 122. 3. *Ephes.* 2. 19. The Argument lyeth thus. If a true Church be a Citie of God, then a Church becomes a Church by Covenant : But every true Church is a Citie of God. *Ergo.*

The Assumption is proved by the Scriptures forealledged. The Consequence of the Proposition is plaine in reason, for every Citie is united by some Covenant among themselves, the Citizens are received into *jus Civitatis,* or right of Citie priviledges, by some
Covenant

Covenant or Oath; And therefore it is so likewise in this Citie of God the Church; and men become Citizens of the Church by solemne Covenant.

The third Argument may be drawne from the meanes of re- *Argu.3.* forming and restoring a Church when it is corrupted, which is by entring into Covenant a new with God, 2 *Chron.*15.10. & 29.10. & *Neh.*9.38. & 10.28,29 *Jer.*50 4,5. The reason may be ta- ken thus: If a Church decayed is to be restored and reformed by renuing Covenant with God, then it was instituted and erected at the first by way of Covenant: The reason of which Consequence is, because abuses and corruptions are to be reformed by bringing things back to the first Institution: Thus Christ reformes the abu- ses of marriage, by bringing them to the first Institution of that Ordinance; *From the beginning it Was not so*, Mat. 19 8. And thus *Paul* reformeth the Abuses of the Lords Supper, by telling them what was the first Institution thereof, 1 *Cor.*11.23 &c. And thus the Lord Jesus calling on the declining Church of *Ephesus* for re- formation, *bids her remember from whence shee is fallen, and repent and doe her first workes*, Rev. 2.5.

Now the Assumption is plaine from the Texts above alledged, that at the reforming of a Church, there is to be a renuing of Co- venant; and thence it follows, that at the first erecting of a Church, there was the making of a Covenant with God, for els this renu- ing of Covenant would not have been the way to reforme it.

The fourth Argument is taken from that which doth dissolve *Argu.* 4. a Church, which is the dissolving or breaking of the Covenant, *Zach.*11.9,10 14. If dissolving the Covenant be that which doth dissolve the Church, then the making of Covenant is that which constitutes a Church. The reason of the Consequence is plaine, because otherwise the Covenant might be dissolved & the Church stand still, if it were not the making of the Covenant that did con- stitute the Church: But if dissipating stones in a building doe dis- solve the house, then the compacting and conjoyning of them is that which makes the house; If separation of soule and body be that which destroyes the man, that then we say he is not: it must needs be the uniting of them, that did constitute & make the man: and so it is in this case. And that dissolving the Covenant is that which dissolves a Church, is plaine from the Text alledged, *Zach.*11, where the breaking of the two staves, of beautie and

bands,

bands, that is, the unchurching of the Jewes, is interpreted to be the breaking of the Covenant that God had made with that people, and the brotherhood that was between *Judah* and *Israel.*

Argu.5. The fifth Argument is taken from the distinction which God hath appointed amongst Churches, and the confounding of all Churches into one, if there be not this Covenant to distinguish them. If Churches be distinct Societies, and may not be confounded, then Churches are compacted and combined by Covenant: But the former is true. *Ergo.*

That Churches are distinct Societies, is plaine in the Scripture, where we have mention of many Churches in one Countrey or Province, *Gal.* 1. 1. 1 *Thes.* 2. 14. Of seven Churches in Asia, *Rev.* 1. 4. and of all the Churches, 1 *Cor.* 14. 33. *Rev.* 2. 23. *Ephesus* is not *Smyrna,* nor *Smyrna* is not *Thyatira,* nor either of them *Pergamus,* but each one distinct of themselves, having Officers of their owne, which did not belong to others : vertues of their owne for which others are not praised, corruptions of their owne, for which others are not blamed ; If it were not thus, then when *Laodicea* is condemned for lukewarmenesse, or *Ephesus* for declining, all the rest should be reproved also : And when *Philadelfia* is praised, all the rest should be praised also, which we see is otherwise. Now from hence the Consequence is certaine, that therefore they are combined by some Covenant each one amongst themselves ; for there is nothing els without this that wil sufficiently distinguish them. The Spirit of God and Faith in their hearts, is common to all Christians under heaven, and in heaven also, and therefore this is not the thing that makes distinction. Nor is it habitation in the same Towne together, for that may be common to such Christians as are not of this Church, and usually is to many that are no Christians. As it is with Companies in *London* ; as the Company of Goldsmiths, &c. that many others dwell in the same Towne with them, yea it may be in the same streete that are not of their Company : and therefore it is not meerely habitation that doth distinguish them from others, but some combination and agreement amongst themselves ; So it is not habitation in the same Towne that distinguisheth Churches, and Church members from other men, but their mutuall agreement and combination and joyning themselves together in an holy Covenant with God.

" If

Object.

" *If the Spirit of God and Faith in their hearts cannot distinguish one*
" *Church from another, because these are common to them all, then how*
" *can Covenant distinguish them, sith all Churches are joyned by Cove-*
" *nant one as well as another ?*

It is not a Covenant simply or a Covenant in generall that doth *Answer.*
constitute a Church, or distinguish one Church from another,
but a Covenant with application and appropriation to these persons. Even as it is in marriage, though all married couples be united by Covenant, and a Covenant wherein one couple promiseth
the same duties that another couple doth. yet a Covenant with application and appropriation of the duties covenanted to this man
and this woman in particular, such a Covenant is the very thing
that make a couple, man and wife together. and gives them mutuall power over each other, as husband and wife, and puts a distinction between them and all other men and women in the world.
And so it is in this case ; a Covenant to performe Church-duties
with application and appropriation to such persons, is the very
thing that constitutes a Church, and distinguisheth one Church
from another.

And thus much concerning the former of the two particulars,
to shew the use of Church-Covenant, *viz.* that it is that whereby
a company doe become a Church.

The second particular is this, that taking hold of the Covenant,
or joyning in it, is that which makes a particular person a member
of a Church. And this followes upon the former, and that may
be the first Argument to prove it.

If joyning in Covenant be that which makes a company to be- *Argu. 1.*
come a Church, then taking hold of that Covenant is requisite to
make a particular person become a member of the Church : But
the first is true, as hath been shewed before ; Therefore the second
is true also : If compacting and conjoyning of stones and pieces
of Timber, be that that makes an house, then a particular stone
cannot become a part of that house, till it be compacted and conjoyned to the rest : But the former is true, even in the Church of
God, which is the spirituall Spouse and Citie of God, living stones,
Christians, beleevers must be compacted together, and builded up
together, *Ephes* 2. 21. 22. *Psal* 122. 3. and therefore the latter is
true also, that a particular Christian becomes a member of the
Church, a part of that building by being combined with the rest.

A

Argu. 2.   A second Argument may be drawne from the Scripture, *Isa.* 56. 3, 6, 7. *Let not the sonne of the stranger, that hath joyned himselfe to the Lord, speake, saying, the Lord hath utterly separated me from his people, &c. The sonnes of the strangers that joyne themselves to the Lord, to serve him, &c. and take hold of my Covenant, even them will I bring to my holy mountaine, and make them joyfull in my house of Prayer, &c.* Concerning which Scripture, note three things to the present purpose. First, That these strangers were members of Christ, true beleevers, joyned to God by Faith; for it is said, *they have joyned themselves to the Lord, v. 3 & v. 6.* that they loved the name of the Lord, served him, and kept his Sabbaths, *v. 6.* and yet for all this they were not as yet joyned as members of the visible Church, for if they had been ioyned, there would have been no cause for such a complaint, *the Lord hath separated me from his people, v. 3.* Besides, bringing them into the Church as members, and granting them the priviledge of members, is promised as a reward and blessing upon this their joyning to the Lord by faith and obedience, *v. 7.* And therefore it is not the same, but a distinct thing from it; the one being promised as a reward and blessing upon the other. Secondly, The Lord promiseth that he will make them members of his Church: *Them will I bring to my holy mountaine, and make them joyfull in my house of Prayer.* Thirdly, That among other things requisite to make them members, this was one, *viz.* the taking hold of that Covenant which was between the Church of *Israel* and God, *v. 6.* So that hence we may gather, that men may be members of Christ, joyned to the Lord by faith and love, and yet for the present not be members of the visible Church: And that when God is so gracious to true beleevers, as to make them members of his visible Church, it is requisite that they joyne in Covenant before.

Object.   " *But might not faith in Christ, beleeving in heart on the God of Israel, be all the taking hold of the Covenant that is here meant.*

Answer.   Not so, but over and above that, here is also meant their open profession of their Faith in the God of *Israel,* and open binding of themselves by Covenant to all such duties of faith and obedience, as God required of the Church of *Israel,* and the members thereof. Now distinctly take the Answer to this Objection in three or foure particular Propositions. First, There was a Covenant between the Church of *Israel* and God, *Exod.* 19 5, 6, 7, 8. *Ezek* 16. 8. *Deut.* 29. 10. &c. Secondly, This Covenant was mutuall; not onely

onely a promife on Gods part to be their God, and to take them
for his people, but alfo reciprocally on their part to give up themfelves unto God to be his people, and to doe the dutie of people to
their God ; The Covenant is not meerely to receive from God,
and promife nothing back againe to him ; nor doth God binde
himfelfe therein, and leave men at libertie, but it is mutuall on both
parts, as thefe Scriptures declare ; *Gen.* 17. 1. *Exod.* 19.7. 8. *Deut.* 5.
27. & 26. 16, 17. *Hof.* 2. 23. & *Zach.* 13. 9. Thirdly, Hereupon
it followes, that if men had not promifed, and alfo performed, in
fome meafure of truth, the duties of Faith and obedience unto
God, they had not taken hold of the Covenant, but had difcovenanted themfelves, notwithftanding all the promifes of God unto
their Fathers or others. Thus though God promifed *Abraham* to
be a God to him, and to his feede in their generations, *Gen.* 17. 7.
yet the *Iſhmaelites* and *Edomites* defcending from *Abraham*, were
difcovenanted by not promifing nor performing thofe duties of
Faith and obedience , which God required on the peoples part :
when a Covenant containes promifes on Gods part, and duties alfo on mans, he doth not take hold of the Covenant that takes one
part, and leaves another. Fourthly, To beleeve what God promifed in the Covenant for his part, and to promife in a private way
the duties of obedience on mans part, was not fufficient to make
thefe ftrangers members of the Church, but they muft doe it openly and in the view of the Church, elfe the Church cou'd have had
no warrant to have admitted fuch into their Fellowfhip, if their
faith and obedience had not been vifibly profeffed, *Exod.* 12. 43.
48 2 *Chron.* 23. 19.

And in as much as the Covenant was mutuall, when thefe ftrangers did manifeft their taking hold of the Covenant, they manife-
fted and profeffed both Faith and obedience, both that they beleeved what God promifed, and that they would be obedient to what
he required ; If any fhould have claimed Church fellowfhip, faying, I beleeve the promifes, but would not binde himfe to any
duties of Evangelicall obedience, this had been a taking hold of the
Covenant by the haives, a taking of one part of it in feeming and
pretence, and a leaving of another ; but it would not have been
fufficient to have brought a man into the fellowfhip of the church :
Such of the Congregation of *Iſrael* as would not come to *Hieruſalem* to enter into Covenant, were to be feparated from the Church

in the dayes of *Ezra*, *Ezra* 10. 8. And therefore such as being
strangers should refuse to enter into it, could not be admitted into
the Church ; So that the taking hold of Gods Covenant, which
is there required to make these strangers members of the Church,
is a beleeving in heart on the God of *Israel*, and an open profession that they did beleeve, and likewise a promise of obedience or
subjection unto the God of *Israel*, and an open professing of such
obedience and subjection ; and that is the joyning in Covenant
which we stand for, before a man can be a member of a Church,
even an open profession of Faith and of Obedience.

*Argu.*3.   A third Argument is taken from those Scriptures which shew
that men become members by being added to the Church, or being joyned to them, *Act.* 2. 47. & 5. 13. & 9. 26. If men become
members of the Church by being added or joyned, then joyning
in Covenant (or professing of subjection to the Gospel or Covenant of God) is that whereby a man becomes a member of a
Church : But the former is true, as appeares by the Scriptures forementioned, and therefore the latter is true also.

But all the doubt in this Argument will be concerning the consequence of the *Major* Proposition ; but that may be made good
by this reason, and the confirmation of it, *viz.* that a man cannot
be added or joyned to the Church by any other meanes without
this joyning in Covenant. The truth of which Assertion will appeare by shewing the insufficiency of all other means, without this
joyning in Covenant, and that may be done in Answer to the
Objections ensuing.

*Object.*1.   " *When men were added to the Church, it may be, no more is meant*
" *but that God did convert them and worke Faith in their hearts, and that*
" *converting of them was the adding of them to the* Church.

Answer.   This cannot be all ; for, first, *Saul* was converted and had faith
wrought in his heart, and yet he was not at the first received for a
member of the Church at *Hierusalem* (though he assayed to be
joyned unto them,) till they were better satisfied in his spirituall
estate by the testimony of *Barnabas*, *Act.* 9. 26, 27, 28. And those
strangers, *Isa.* 56. (as was said before) were joyned to the Lord
by being converted, and having Faith wrought in their hearts,
and yet they doe lament it with griefe, that they were not joyned
as members to the visible Church : *The Lord hath separated me from
his people,* say they, *ver.* 3. The old saying is true concerning the
                                                              visible

vifible Church, *There are many wolves within, and many sheepe with-out.* Secondly, Thofe that were joyned were beleevers before they joyned; for it is faid, *divers were added,* ver. 14. Thirdly, Thofe that were added to the Church, were added and joyned to them by fuch an act as others durft not put forth, *Act. 5. 13. Of the reft durft no man joyne unto them,* and therefore it was not by the irrefiftable act of God in converting of them, but by fome voluntary act of their owne choice and confent; for Gods converting grace depends not upon mans daring, or not daring to receive it. If to be joyned be no more but to be converted, then when it is faid, *Some durft not be joyned,* the meaning fhould be, they durft not be converted, nor fuffer Faith to be wrought in them; which is groffe Arminianifme, fufpending the converting grace of God upon the free will of the creature. Fourthly, And as this joyning which others durft not doe, cannot be meant of being converted; So if it be well confidered, what the thing was wherein they durft not joyne, it may appeare that it was nothing els but this, that they durft not agree, and engage themfelves to be of their body and focietie; that is, they durft not joyne in Covenant with them. For it cannot be meant of dwelling in the Towne with them, for this they both durft doe and did : nor is it onely of joyning to heare the Word in their affembly, for this alfo they durft doe, and many did it in great multitudes, fo that many by hearing the Word became beleevers, and were added to the Lord both of men and women, *ver.* 14. at this very time when it is faid of fome they durft not joyne unto them : Nor is it of joyning to them in affection, or approbation of their way, for this they alfo durft doe and did expreffe fo much in magnifying and commending them, when yet they durft not joyne unto them, *ver.* 13. Which magnifying of them doth imply that they heard their doctrine, and faw their practife, and approved it, and highly commended them for the fame : Wherefore feeing this joyning, which fome durft not doe, cannot be meant of being converted, nor of joyning in habitation, nor of joyning in affection, nor in hearing the Word in their Affembly, nor of approbation, and expreffions that way, it remaineth that it muft be meant of joyning in that neere relation of Church-fellowfhip amongft them, fo as to be engaged by voluntary confent and agreement to be members of their Church. Fiftly, If joyning to the Church, were no more but to be con-

C 2

verted,

verted, then he that were converted were joyned as a member of every visible Church throughout the world, which were a great confusion of that Order, and distinction of Churches, which the Lord hath appointed.

Obj. 2.   " *Men may be joyned to the Church, in heartie affection and love, and* " *yet without any Covenant.*

Answ.   True, but this will not make them members of that Church, for then *Saul* was a member of the Church at *Hierusalem*, afore he was joyned a member, for he was joyned to them in heartie affection afore, and therefore assayed to joyne as a member; and so were they that durst not joyne, *Act.* 5. 13. yea then a man should be a member of many Churches, yea of all Christian Churches in the world; for he is to love them, and beare heartie affection to them all; The true members of the Churches in *England* are united in heartie affection, to the Churches in *Scotland*, in *Holland*, in *Fraunce*, in *New-England*, &c. And yet they are not members of all these Churches, nor subject to their censures as members are.

Obj. 3.   " *But the reason of that is because they doe not dwell among them in* " *the same Towne.*

Answer.   Neither would habitation with them in the same Towne, make a man a member of the Church there, if there be no more then so. Suppose *Saul* to have dwelt in the same house afore his conversion in which he dwelt after, which is not unpossible nor unlikely; yet we see he was no member of the Church at *Hierusalem*, afore his conversion, no nor of some time after, though he might have dwelt in an house in the midst of the Christians, and Church-members there. The members of the *Dutch* and *French* Churches in *London*, or other Townes in *England*, are not members of the *English*-Congregations or Churches, no more then the *English* are of theirs, and yet they dwell promiscuously together in the same Streete of the same Towne. Towne-dwelling would not make a man a free-man of a Company in *London*, or some other Corporation; for many others dwell in the Towne with them; yea it may be in the same streete, that are not free of their Company, and so it is in this case.

Object.4.   " *But the reason why such as dwell in Towne with the Church, are* " *not members thereof, may be, because they frequent not their Assem-* " *blies.*

                                                        Idiots

Idiots and Infidells might come into the publick meetings a-mong the *Corinthians*, 1 *Cor.* 14. 23, 24, 25. yet Idiots and Infi-dells were not therefore members of the Church. And *Saul* after his conversion might have come in among the Church in time of publick duties, and have seene and heard all that they had done: yet this would not have made him of one body with them. Some *Indians, Moores,* and other naturall persons come into our meet-ings in *New - England,* some of their owne accord, and others by the Command or Counsell of their Masters and Governours, yet no man can say, that all these are hereby made Church-members. Wherefore seeing neither conversion, nor loving affection, nor cohabitation, nor coming into their meetings, doth joyne a man as a member of the visible Church (for some men have all these, and yet are not members, and others are sometimes members of the visible Churches, and yet want some of these, are hypocrites and want sound conversion) it remaineth therefore that as sound conversion makes a man fit matter for a Church; So profession of his Faith, and of his subjection to the Gospel, and the Churches approbation, and acceptance of him (which is the summe of Church-Covenant) is the formall cause that gives him the being of a member.

" *But joyning doth not alway signifie joyning in Covenant ; Philip joy-* " *ned to the Eunnuchs chariote, and dust to mens feete,* Act. 8. 29. & " *Luke* 10, 11. *and yet there was no Covenant, and therefore men may* " *joyne to the Church without any Covenant.*

The word indeed may expresse any close joyning, whether na-turall, (as the branch is joyned to the Vine, or an arme or other member to the body) or artificiall, as when two stickes were joy-ned to become one in *Ezekiels* hand, *Ezek.* 37. Or when Carpen-ters or Masons doe joyne pieces of stone or Timber together, to make one house, *Neh.* 4. 6. *Ezr.* 4. 12. but is not onely the force of the word that is stood upon. But when joyning is used to ex-presse such joyning, wherein a man voluntarily takes on him a new relation, there it alwayes implyes a Covenant, whether the relation be morall and civill, or religious and Ecclesiasticall : We speake of voluntary relation, for there are naturall relations, as be-tweene parents and children : and these need no Covenant, there is no Covenant to make a man a Parent, or a childe ; There are also violent relations, as between Conquerour and Captives, and

in

in thefe there is no Covenant neither ; but others are voluntary, and thefe alwayes imply a Covenant, and are founded therein, whether they be morall and civill (as between husband and wife, *Pro.* 2. 17. between Mafter and fervants, *Luk.* 15. 15. between Prince and fubject, between Partners in Trade, 2 *Chro.* 20. 35, 36, 37. where the Covenant or agreement is, that men fhall bare fuch a fhare of charges, and receive fuch a fhare of profits :) or religious, as between Minifter and people, between the Church and the members : all thefe are done by way of Covenant. A man cannot joyne himfelfe to a woman as her husband, but by way of Covenant : A man cannot joyne himfelfe to another as a fervant, or apprentife, but by way of Covenant ; And fo may we fay of all the reft ; nor into any body corporate, but by the fame way and means. If men be united into a body politick or incorporate, a man cannot be faid to be joyned to them by meere heartie affection, unleffe withall he joynes himfelfe unto them by fome Contract or Covenant. Now of this nature is every particular Church, a body incorporate, 1 *Cor.* 12. 27. *Yee are the body of Chriff, &c.* and hath power to caft out, 1 *Cor.* 5. 13. and to forgive and receive in Penitents, 2 *Cor.* 2. 7. 8 as a body incorporate ; and therefore he that will joyne unto them, muft doe it by way of Covenant or Agreement ; and fo this Anfwer to this Objection, may be a fourth Argument to prove the point in hand, that joyning in Covenant is that which makes a man, a member of a Church.

Argu. 4.   All voluntary relations, all relations which are neither naturall nor violent, are entred into by way of Covenant.

But he that joynes into a Church as a member, or enters into a Church, doth take upon him fuch a relation ; Therefore joyning to a Church as a member, is by way of Covenant.

Argu. 5.   A fifth Argument may be drawne from the power which all Churches, Officers and members, have over all their members in the Lord. If all Churches, Officers, and members, have power in the Lord over all their members, then joyning in Covenant is neceffary to make a man a member of a Church, but the former is true, therefore the latter is true alfo.

The Affumption in this Argument, that all Churches have power over their members, is proved from 1 *Cor.* 5. 4. 5. 13. where the Apoftle reproveth the *Corinthians* for fuffering the In-
ceftuous

cestuous man amongst them, and commands them to deliver him to Satan, and cast him out from amongst them. Now this he would not have done, if they had had no power over him, or if there had been any roome for them to say, wee have nothing to doe with him, wee have no power over him. And the same is prooved in other Scriptures also; as, *Mat.* 18. 17. *Psal.* 149. 6. 7, 8, 9.

And the Consequence of the *Major* Proposition, *viz.* that then members doe engage themselves by Covenant, is proved by this reason; That Churches have no power over such as have not engaged themselves by Covenant, and committed power unto them, by professing to be subject to all the Ordinances of Christ amongst them.

The truth whereof may appeare by two Reasons:

First, Because all Christians have power and right, *jure divino,* to choose their owne Officers to whom they commit their soules, *Act.* 6. *&* 1. *&* 14. 23. where the word χειροτονησαντες, imports choosing by Election: and so the word is used and translated, 2 *Cor.* 8. 19. *he was chosen by the Churches, &c.* It is not ministeriall gifts that makes a man a Minister to every Church, nor investeth him with spirituall power over them, nor though he dwell amongst them, unlesse they call him, and he accept of that call: And as they have power to choose their Officers, so likewise to choose their brethren according to God, *Rom.* 14. 1. Now if they have power to choose their Officers and brethren, then none can have power over them as Officers and brethren, without their owne consent, and whom they never chose, nor promised by any Covenant or Engagement to be subject to the Lord.

Secondly, If the Church should exercise any Act of Church-power over such a man as never entred into Covenant with them (suppose to Excommunicate him for whoredome or drunkennesse, or the like) the man might protest against their Act, and their Sentence, as *Coram non judice.* and they could not justifie their proceedings, if indeed there have passed no Covenant or Engagement between him and them. If he shall say, you have nothing to doe to passe Sentence or Censure upon me, I am none of your Church, but of another Church; Suppose in *Holland,* in *France, &c.* and I am onely here now for Merchandise sake, or upon some other occasion: what shall they say to stop his mouth, if there never
ver

ver paſſed any Covenant between him and them.

Object. " *But Miniſters have power over the people by the word of God,* " Heb. 13. 17. 1 Theſ. 5. 12. 1 Tim. 5. 17. *and not by mens engaging* " *themſelves by Covenant.*

Anſwer. But what is it that makes men Miniſters to ſuch a people, Officers to ſuch a Church, or maketh them ſheepe of my flocke? Is it not thoſe Scriptures that makes every man a Paſtour, or Teacher, or Ruler to a people, unleſſe they call him to that Office; and then in ſo doing they Covenant and Engage themſelves to be ſubject to him in the Lord, and then thoſe Scriptures take hold on them. One might as well ſay, it is not the Covenanting of a wife to her husband that gives him power over her, but the Word of God; For as the Word of God commands people to obey their Miniſters, ſo it commands *wives to be ſubject to their husbands,* Epheſ. 5. 22. And yet all men know, a man cannot take this woman for his wife but by Covenant. So that if ſhee once makes her ſelfe a wife by her owne voluntary Covenant, then the word of God takes hold on her, and bindes her to doe the duties of a wife : but if ſhee, hath made no Covenant, the man hath no power over her as her husband, neither is ſhee his wife ; So if men once make themſelves members of ſuch a Church, ſheepe of ſuch a mans flocke, by their own voluntary Covenant, then the word of God takes hold of them, and bindes them to doe the duties of members to their fellow-brethren, and of people to their Paſtours or Miniſters. But if they never choſe ſuch a man to be their Miniſter, nor Covenanted to be ſubject to him in the Lord, he then can have no power over them as a Miniſter unto them, becauſe they have right to choſe their owne Miniſters.

Argu. 6. A ſixth Argument may be taken from the diſtinction that is between members, and not members. If there be by the word of God a diſtinction, between members of the Church and ſuch as are no members, then joyning in Covenant is neceſſary to the being of a member ; but the former is true, as appeares 1 Cor. 5. 12. Some are within, and may be judged by the Church, and others are without, and may not : and therefore the latter is true alſo. And the reaſon of the Conſequence is becauſe there is nothing elſe without this joyning in Covenant, that can ſufficiently diſtinguiſh them ; It is not Faith and Grace in their hearts, for ſome men are members of the viſible Church, and yet have no

Grace,

Grace, and others may have Grace, and yet be no members; and therefore this is not the thing that doth diſtinguiſh them, nor is it affection, nor cohabitation, nor every approbation of the Word of God, and the wayes of his Church, nor comming into their Aſſemblies to heare the Word; But theſe things were touched before, and therefore may be here the more briefly paſſed over.

And ſo much ſhall ſuffice to have ſpoken of the ſecond particular, concerning the uſe of Church-Covenant, that it is by joyning therein that a particular perſon becomes a member of a Church.

But here it will be needfull to remove ſundry Objections, which may ſeeme to ſome to be of great weight againſt Church-Covenant, that ſo by the removing of them, the truth may be the more cleared, to fuller ſatisfaction, if it be the will of God.

" *Church-Covenant is a Terme that is not found in Scripture.* Objeƈt.1.

Firſt, So is Sacrament, Trinitie, &c. and yet thoſe termes may Anſwer. be lawfully uſed, becauſe the thing meant thereby is found.

Secondly, But ſeeing the Covenant is between the Lord and his Church, as the two parties that are confederate, it is all one whether it be called the Lords Covenant, or the Church-Covenant : As when *Mamre, Aver,* & *Eſchol* were confederate with *Abraham,* Gen. 14. 13. might not one truely ſay, *Abraham* was confederate with them? Relatives doe mutually put and eſtabliſh one another.

Thirdly, The Scripture allowes both the Lords Covenant with the Church, *Eze.*16.8.& the peoples covenant or Saints covenant, or Churches Covenant with him, *Deut.*29.12.*Pſal.*50.5.*Jer.*50.5.

Fourthly, There is good reaſon for both the words; both the Lords Covenant, and the Church-Covenant, becauſe both are confederate; And for that of Church-Covenant, there is this reaſon alſo, *viz.* to diſtinguiſh it from other Covenants, as a marriage-Covenant, *Pro.*2.17.and a brotherly Covenant, 1 *Sam.* 20. 8. The Church-Covenant being thus called not onely becauſe they are a Church, or members thereof that make it, but alſo becauſe they enter into it in reference to Church-Eſtate and Church-duties : The duties which they bind themſelves unto in this Covenant being ſuch eſpecially as concern a Church and the members thereof.

" *But this Church-Covenant puts ſome diſparagement upon the Cov-* Objeƈt.2
" *nant of Grace, which every beleever is already entred into with God,*
" *and ſeeme to charge the ſame with inſufficiency ; for every ſecond Cove-*
" *nant doth argue that the firſt was not faultleſſe,* Heb. 8. 7.

D   1. A

Answ.   1. A second Covenant doth argue that the first was not fault-
lesse, where the Covenants are contrary one to another, as the
covenant of Grace, and the covenant of works are, and so it is
most true, that the bringing in of the free Covenant of Grace did
argue that righteousnes and life could not be attained by the Law,
or Covenant of works; for if there had been a Law given which
could have given life, verily righteousnesse should have been by
the Law. *Gal.* 3. 21. *Rom.* 8. 3.

    2. But if it be the same Covenant that *is* renewed or made a-
gaine, though upon a new occasion, no man can say that entring
into the same the second time, or a third, or a fourth, doth disanull
the first, or cast disparagement upon the same. The covenant of
works given to *Adam* was not blamed or faulted, because it was
renewed in *Sinai*. The Covenant of Grace was first given to *Adam*
in Paradise after his fall, afterward to *Abraham*, then to the people
of Israel under types and shadows; And againe after the coming
of Christ in the flesh; yet none of these doth disanull the former,
or argue the same to be faulty; and the reason is, because it is still
the same Covenant though renewed upon new occasions; and in
some particulars in some other manner. And the like we say concerning Church-Covenant, or the Covenant which a man makes
when he enters into the Church, *viz.* that it is not another Covenant contrary to the Covenant of Grace, which every beleever is
brought into at his first conversion, but an open profession of a
mans subjection to that very Covenant, specially in the things
which concerne Church estate, into which estate the man is now
entring.

Obj. 3.   " *It is not lawfull to make such a Covenant as the Church-Covenant,*
        " *because it is not in our power to keep it, and we do not know whether*
        " *God will give us power.*

Answ.   This ground is very true, that no man hath power of himselfe
to any thing that good is, but all a mans power and abilitie must
come of God through Christ, 2. *Cor.* 3. 5. *Phil.* 2. 13. *Joh.* 15. 5.
But the inference is not good, that therefore it should be unlawfull
to ento into Church-Covenant: for 1. By the same reason, all promises are unlawfull, and all covenants whatsoever; as the covenant of marriage, the covenant of service, yea and the personall
covenant of Grace, when a particular soule promiseth faith and
new obedience; for there is none of these, no not the covenant of
Marriage,

Marriage, which a man is able of himself to keep, as the adultery of *David* and *Bathsheba,* among others, doth plainly prove.

2. God hath promised to give power to them that in self-deniall seek it of him, and trust to his promise for it. *Ezek.* 36. 27. *Jer.* 31. 33. *Rom.* 6. 14. *Jer.* 32. 40. The true inference therefore from this ground, from mans disabilitie to performe were this, that therefore a man should not enter into Church Covenant in his owne strength, for that was *Peters* fault in promising not to deny Christ, but to die with him rather : but Church-Covenant, as also all other promises, should be entred into, in an humble looking up to Christ Jesus for help and assistance to performe. *Thou therefore my sonne, be strong in the grace that is in Christ Jesus,* 2. *Tim.* 2. 1.

" *God disalloweth covenants of mans making* (and so our *Church-* Obj. 4.
" *Covenant*) *in those words, But not by thy Covenant.* Ezek. 16. 61.

God doth not reprove them there for making Covenant, for *Answ.* then he were contrary to himselfe, who elsewhere called them to do it, *Exod.* 29. *Deut.* 29. and commended them for it, *Psal.* 50. 5. Yea and in that very place of *Ezek.* 16. acknowledgeth a Covenant betweene him and them, *ver.* 60. 62. But the meaning is, he would do them good, but not for their good keeping the Covenant of works, for they had very sinfully broken it, *ver.* 59 but even as he saith elsewhere, not for their sakes, or for their righteousnesse, *Ezek.* 36. 32. *Deut.* 9. 4, 5, 6. But what force is there in this arguing, *viz.* If God will do us good, but not for our good keeping the covenant of works, then it is not lawfull to promise obedience to the covenant of Grace, in such things as concerne Church estate ; All men may easily see that here is a plaine *non sequitur.*

" *This entring into Covenant may keep out many good men from joyn-* Obj. 5.
" *ing to the Churches, because they are not satisfied about it: and therefore*
" *it is better laid aside.*

It is not impossible, but good men may for a time be unsatisfied *Answ.* about it, till they understand the nature and use of it, and yet the thing be warrantable enough for all that in the sight of God ; the Tribes were troubled at the Altar set up upon the banks of Jordan by the two Tribes and an halfe, till they understood the intent and use of it, and for what purpose it was erected : and then they were satisfied. *Josh.* 22. And the same may be said of *Peters* eating with the Gentiles, which at the first was very offensive to them of the

circumcision,

circumcifion, till they underftood what *Peter* had to fay for his defence therein, and then they refted well fatisfied, *Act.* 11.

But if men underftand what the Church-Covenant is, there is no reafon that good men fhould be troubled at it ; it being nothing elfe but a promife of obedience unto the Gofpel of Chrift, or of fuch duties as the Gofpel requireth of all Chriftians in Church-eftate : For, will good men refufe to obey the Gofpel, or fubmit to the ordinances of Chrift ? or will they refufe to profeffe and promife fo much ? If a man underftand what it is, and what we meane by it, and yet refufe to enter into it when he hath opportunitie thereto, fuch refufing is no part of his goodneffe, but is to be reckoned amongft his corruptions ; It is ignorance at the beft, and if not fo, then it may be perverfeneffe of will, or fome want of will to performe obedience to the Gofpel. And furely there is fmal hope that fuch would yeeld fubjection and obedience to the Gofpel, who do refufe to profeffe or promife it.

Obj. 6.   " But the Scripture, Act. 2. 41. *tels of joyning to the Church with-* " *out any Covenant. For it was not poffible that* 3000. *fhould enter into* " *covenant in one day.*

Anfw.   Two things may be faid in Anfwer to this Objection.

Firft, that 3000. were not fo many, but that joyning in Covenant might eafily be done by them all, in one day. For, 1. it was at Penticoft, at which time of the yeer the dayes were at the longeft : And, 2. the Scripture tels us, that *David* made a Covenant with all the Tribes of Ifrael in one day, 2. *Sam.* 5 1, 2, 3. The Articles of the covenant betweene *David* and the Tribes, and fo betweene this 3000. and the Lord might be openly declared, and they both the one and the other might by fome figne or other, expreffe their confent thereunto in one day.

Secondly, as joyning in Covenant is a thing that might be done, fo it is more then probable that indeed it was done, by thofe 3000. foules. For it is faid, *ver.* 41. *that they gladly received the word,* that is, they openly profeffed that they did with all their hearts receive it, for this receiving of the Word is noted as a condition, upon which they were admitted to baptifme, and therefore it was not onely an inward receiving of it in their hearts, but alfo an open profeffing that they did receive it ; for an inward receiving of it in their hearts, without an open profeffing thereof outwardly, would not have been fufficient for the admitting of them unto Baptifme.

Now

Now this Word which they received was an exhortation to Repentance for finne, and to Faith in the promife, *ver.* 38 39. and to obedience in fevering themfelves from others, and faving themfelves from that untoward generation, *ver.* 40. And therefore when they openly profeffed, that they gladly received this word, there was an open profeffing of their Repentance for finne, *ver.* 40. of their Faith in the promife, and of obedience to the Commandement, which is nothing elfe, but the very fumme of Church-Covenant: yea, and further, their very preparation to this repentance, faith and obedience, in that true compunction and forrow of foul, was alfo openly made manifeft. *ver.* 37.

" *But yet there would not be fuch long narrations, of every one feve-* Reply.
" *rally as now are ufed, when men do enter into Church-Covenant, when*
" *each one makes a good long fpeech, in the profeffion of his Faith and Re-*
" *pentance.*

When the thing is certaine, as was fhewed before, that they did *Anfw.* openly profeffe repentance, faith and obedience, it is not difference in the length or largeneffe of their fpeeches in expreffing of themfelves, that can make any difference in the thing: *Majus & minus non diverfificant fpeciem.* And we denie not but they might be briefer, becaufe there was not fuch need they fhould be long in regard of fome difference betweene them and us, their time and ours: Firft there were the Apoftles prefent to heare their confeffions, and to judge thereof, who were men of very good difcerning, and therefore briefer expreffing of mens felves might fuffice; whereas the beft Chriftians, yea the beft Minifters amongft us are not to be compared to the Apoftles; and therefore as we need more time for ftudy, and for preparation for our Sermons then they did: fo likewife we need more time to heare, and try the foundneffe of mens repentance towards God, and faith towards our Lord Jefus Chrift. Yet this we may adde withall, that if the Apoftles and thofe primative Chriftians, men of fuch excellent difcerning were fometimes deceived, and could not alwayes fo difcern, but that fome Hypocrites would creep into the Church: as the example of *Ananias* and *Saphira* doth witneffe; how much more need is there, that the Churches of God in thefe dayes (being far inferiour to them) fhould be very watchfull and circumfpect in

trying

trying the fpirituall eftates of them that offer to come into the
Church?

Secondly, their times alfo differed from ours : for their Chrifti-
anitie was a matter of reproach and danger of excommunication,
Joh. 9. 22. of imprifonment, *Act*. 4. 3. and 5. 18. and the like.
And therefore to fee men now to make open profeffion of their
faith in Chrift Jefus, whofe fervants and difciples were fo hated,
and who himfelfe but a while before was crucified, this was not an
ordinarie matter : and therefore in words, men might be the briefer
when they came to be received into the Church : But our times in
New England do not perfecute Chrift, and Chriftians, and Chriftian
Churches, but countenance them, and protect them ; and therefore there is more need now to be more ftudious in examination
of mens eftates when they offer themfelves for Church members:
when the Jews were in favour, many of the people of the Land became Jews, *Efth* 8. 17.

Obj. 7.   " *But why is there fo little proofe of this Church-Covenant in the New*
" *Teftament?*

Anfw.   1. Suppofe the New Teftament faid nothing of it, yet it might
have ground fufficient from the Scriptures of the old Teftament;
for if it was Gods revealed will in thofe dayes, that a companie
fhould become a Church, and particular perfons become members
of that Church by way of Covenant, we may be fure it is fo now
likewife, unleffe covenanting were peculiar to the Jewifh Pædigo-
gic; indeed if it had never been ufed in thofe times, but were fome
new ordinance, peculiar to the dayes of the New Teftament, in
fuch cafes alfo a ground from the Scriptures of the New Teftament were neceffarie, as there is in all fuch things wherein there is
any change or variation, from what was ufed in thofe times afore
Chrift, as that there fhould not be Nationall Churches, but congregationall, and not one vifible Church, but many, that there
fhould be baptifme, and the Lords Supper : thefe are matters that
are not found in the old Teftament, nor were appointed to be ufed
in thofe dayes, and therefore we muft have warrant for them in
the New, and fo we have. But for the Covenant it is otherwife, it
is no new ordinance peculiar to the dayes of the Gofpel, nor any
Leviticall ordinance peculiar to the Jewifh Pedigogie; and therefore the Scriptures of the Old Teftament that give warrant for it,
may be fufficient as hath been fhewed afore.

2. And

2. And yet there is not wanting good warrant for it, that it ought to be ufed, in the dayes of the New Teftament. For, 1. the Prophets do foretell it, *Ifa.* 56. 6, 7. and 44.5. and *Jer.* 50.5. *Ezek.* 20. 37. and in fundrie other places, to omit the reft at this time, becaufe fome of them have been fpoken of before ; Onely let thofe words of *Ifa.* 44. 5. be well confidered, and fee if they do not plainly hold forth that in the dayes of the New Teftament, men fhould openly profeffe their faith, and folemnly bind themfelves by Covenant to be the Lords people, one fhall fay, I am the Lords, and another fhall call himfelf by the name of *Jacob*, and another fhall fubfcribe with his hand, and firname himfelf by the name of *Ifrael.* Thefe words are fo plaine for open profeffing of faith in the Lord, and open binding of mens felves by Covenant unto him, as we conceive nothing need be more.

2. The Apoftles do fufficiently teftifie, that fuch a thing was practifed in their dayes, elfe how fhould we underftand that fellowfhip in the Gofpel in its full latitude and breadth, *Phil.* 1.5. if this combining into Church fellowfhip be no part thereof ; yea when it is faid, *they continued ftedfaftly*, or as the word ἦσαν προσκαρτεροῦντες, may well be tranflated, *they ftrongly did cleave together*, or hold together in fuch a Fellowfhip, which was not preaching and hearing the doctrine of the Apoftles, nor Sacraments, nor Prayer, but a thing diftinct from all thefe. If this combining themfelves into a fpirituall fellowfhip and focietie of Church-ftate be no part thereof, we know not how to underftand it, nor what that fellowfhip fhould meane ; If Doctrine, and Sacraments, and Prayer had not been particularly mentioned, in the fame place, it might have been thought that the Fellowfhip in which they fo fteadfaftly clave together had been no more, but their coming together to obferve thefe faid ordinances, and their communion therein. But when all thefe are particularly mentioned, and Fellowfhip mentioned among them, as a thing diftinct from the reft, we may not confound it with the reft. We might as well fay, that by doctrine is meant Sacraments, and by Sacraments is meant Prayer; as to fay that by Fellowfhip is meant nothing elfe but the exercife of doctrine, and Sacraments, and Prayer. And if thefe as they are diftinctly named, be diftinct ordinances, and may not be confounded, then Fellowfhip being named in the fame manner imports fomething diftinct from them all, and may not be confounded

with

with them, nor with any of them, no more then the other may
be confounded one with another. And if so, then as this Fellowship may import, the communion of their gift and goods one for
the helpe of another, so it must first of all imply a combining of
themselves into Church-state by mutuall agreement, consent, or
covenant.

Furthermore, when the Apostle writeth, that by experience of
the *Corinthians* liberall contribution to the poore Saints, men glo-
rified God for their professed subjection to the Gospel of Christ,
2. *Cor.* 9. 13. he plainly imployes thereby, that the *Corinthians*
had made a profession or promise of such subjection to the Gospel as did comprehend this particular of distributing to the necessitie of the Saints, among other things. And their liberall di-
stribution which he there speaks of, was looked at as one point
of their reall performance of that subjection to the Gospel, which
they had before professed, and promised. Now the Church Covenant is nothing else, but the professing or promising of such subjection, and therefore this place is another proofe of Church-
Covenant. Besides, it hath been shewed afore in *Argument* 3.
that those places which speake of being added to the Church, of
joyning, or assaying to joyne unto the Church, *Act.* 2. 47. and
5 13. and 9. 26. are not expounded according to the full meaning
of them, when they are understood of any other joyning, if joyning in Covenant be left out. And therefore the Scriptures of the
New Testament do beare good witnesse unto Church-Covenant, though, as we said before, the Scriptures of the Old Testament might have been sufficient if the New Testament had spoken nothing of it.

Obj. 8.   " But *Baptisme makes men members of the visible Church, and there-*
" *fore the Covenant is needlesse.*

Answ.   This is answered in the Answer to the fourth of the 32. Questions, where it is shewed at large that Baptisme is a seale of the
Covenant betweene God and the Church, but neither makes the
Church, nor members of the Church, nor alwayes so much as
proves men to be members.

Obj. 9.   " *This Church-Covenant is a late devise, and was not known in anci-*
" *ent time, and therefore is to be rejected.*

Answ.   First, True Antiquitie is that of the Scriptures. Now sith
Church Covenant is warranted by the Scripture, as hath been
                                                        shewed

shewed before in this difcourfe, it cannot be charged to want true
Antiquitie. When the Papifts are wont to charge the doctrine of
Proteftants with Novelty, and fuch as was never heard of before
Luther, the Orthodoxe are wont to anfwer, that if the doctrine
do not agree with the Scripture, then let it be condemned for No-
veltie ; and if it do, it is warranted by the beft Antiquitie , even
the teftimonie of God himfelf who is the Antient of dayes : Our
Faith, faith Doctor *White*, is in all points the fame that is contained in the Scripture, and fo confequently of the fame Antiquitie : and therefore all they that fay it came up but of late, muft
firft prove it contrary to the Word of God, or elfe hold their
peace. *White, Way*, 44. 1. And the fame we fay in this particular of
the Church-Covenant.

Secondly, And yet they that fearch the Stories and Writers of
the times and ages next after the Apoftles, may find fome teftimonie of Church-Covenant in thofe dayes : For inftance, *Juftine
Martyr* in his Apol. 2. makes mention of three things which were
required of all that were admitted into the Church as members,
ἀναγεννήσεις, πίστις, ἣ ὑπόσχεσις, that is regeneration, and foundneffe in
the Faith, and a promife to walke in obedience to the Gofpel.
And generally this was the practife of all thofe times, that never
any man was admitted to Baptifme, nor his children neither , but
they put him to anfwer three queftions, *Abrenuntios?* whereto he
anfwered, *Abrenuntio. Credis ?* whereto his anfwer was , *Credo:*
and *Spondes ?* to which he anfwered, *Spondeo.* So that here was
an open declaration of his Repentance from dead works , and of
the foundneffe of his Faith, in the two firft particulars , and an
open binding himfelf by covenant or promife to walke according
to the Gofpel, in the third. But much needs not to be faid in this
point, unto them that do acknowledge Scripture Antiquitie to be
fufficient, though after times fhould be found to fwerve from the
Rules and Patterns that are therein contained.

" *If Church-Covenant be fo neceffarie, then all the Reformed Churches* **Obj. 10.**
" *are to be condemned as no Churches ; for they have no fuch Co-*
" *venant.*

They that have knowne thofe Churches , not onely by their *Anfw.*
writings, and confeffions of their faith, in Synods and otherwife ;
but alfo by living amongft them, and being eye-witneffes of their
Order, do report otherwife of them, *viz.* that they are combined
together

E

together by folemne Covenant with God and one another. *Zepperus*, fpeaking of the manner, ufed in the reformed Churches, in admitting the children of Church-members to the Lords Table, when they came to age, and have been fufficiently catechifed, and inftructed in the doctrine of Religion, tells us, that fuch children are admitted to the Lords table, by publick profeffion of Faith,and entring into Covenant. " *Confuetum eft*, faith he, *ut qui per æta-* " *tem inque Doctrinâ Catecheticâ profectum ad facram Cœnam primùm* " *admittuntur , fidei confeffionem coram totâ Ecclefiâ publicè edant* " *per parentes aut qui parentum loco funt, juffu miniftri, in Ecclefiæ con-* " *fpectum producti: quòdque in illa confeffione, per Dei gratiam per-* " *ftare, ac, juxta illam, vitam inftituere, infuper etiam difciplinæ Ecclefi-* " *afticæ ultrò ac fponte fuâ fubjicere fefe velint, fpondeant atque ftipu-* " *lentur, Polit. Ecclef. lib. 1. cap. 14. p.* 158. that is, The manner is, " that they who by reafon of age and proficiencie in the doctrine " of Catechifme are firft admitted to the Lords Supper, fhould " publickly before the whole Church make confeffion of their " faith, being brought forth into the fight of the Church by their " parents, or them that are inftead of parents, at the appoint- " ment of the Minifter; and likewife fhould promife and cove- " nant by the grace of God to continue in that Faith which they " have confeffed, and to lead their lives according to it; yea, and " moreover to fubject themfelves freely and willingly to the dif- " cipline of the Church. Thefe words we fee are full and plaine, that children are not in thofe Churches received to the Lords Supper, without perfonall confeffion of Faith, and entring into Covenant before; And if they tooke this courfe with children come to age, there is as much reafon, or more, that the fame courfe fhould be holden with men of yeers, when they are admitted members. And fo the fame *Zepperus*, fpeaking of the confociation of Churches amongft themfelves by mutuall confederation, hath thefe words, which as they may be applyed to the combining of many Churches, fo may they be combining of many members of the fame Church, " Κοινωνια illa των αγιων, *quam in Sym-* " *bolo profitemur Apoftolico, nihil aliud hic requirit, & vult, quam* " *obligationem omnium Ecclefiæ membrorum & confœderationem, &c.* " that is, that communion of Saints which we profeffe in the " Creed, doth require and meane nothing elfe but an obligation " of all the members of the Church, and a binding of them together

" gether by Covenant. *Polit. Eccles. li.* 3 *c.* 8. *p.* 721.

To these testimonies of *Zepperus*, those words may be added of Mr. *Parker* our own countreyman, a man of singular note for learning and holinesse, who also himselfe lived sometimes beyond Sea in the reformed Churches, and there ended his dayes, so that we may safely give the more credit to his testimonie, he having so good meanes truly to know the state and order of those Churches. Now he speaketh of a " *Solennis forma absque qua in* " *Ecclesia alicujus communionem nullus rite recipitur* : of a solemne " forme, without which no man is rightly received into the com-" munion of the Church, hath these words. *Hic mos ille est refor-* " *matarum Ecclesiarum non solum in lapsis restituendis, sed in extraneis,* " *imò quibuscunque recipiendis qui ad habitandum alicubi confident,* " *etsi fortè in Ecclesiâ illius loci quo ante commorabantur, juxta hanc* " *formam admissi prius fuerant. Examinat Presbyterium, plebs consen-* " *tit, quisque testes vitæ suæ secum adfert, vel testimonia saltem : pub-* " *licatur nomen cujusque competentis pro concione, admonetur quisque* " *siquid habeat quod excipiat, ut denunciet presbyteris. Si nihil contrà* " *adferatur, admittitur quidem : sed non nisi solerni pactione cum Deo* " *& cum Ecclesiâ. Spondet verò Ecclesiæ, se ambulaturum prout san-* " *ctam illam communionem decet ; Disciplinæ illius Ecclesiæ subjacere* " *velle, se fratribus illius communionis invigilaturum juxta Christi præ-* " *ceptum, Matth.* 18. 17. *ut præveniantur sanenturque scandala, &* " *illi ad studium bonorum operum provehantur.* That is, This is the " manner of the reformed Churches, not onely in restoring such " as have fallen, but in admitting of strangers, yea of all whoever " they be, who do sit down in any place for habitation, though " perhaps they have been formerly admitted after the same man-" ner in the Church where they have formerly dwelt ; The Pres-" bytery doth examine, the people do consent, every man brings " with him witnesses of his life, or at least wise testimonies : The " name of each one that desires to be a member, is published in the " Assembly, every one is admonished if he have any exception " against the party, to bring it to the Presbytery. It nothing be " brought against him, then indeed he is admitted ; but yet no " otherwise then by a solemne covenant with God and the " Church ; And to the Church he promiseth that he will walk as " becometh that holy Fellowship, that he will be subject to the " discipline of that Church, that he will watch over the brethren

E 2   of

" of that Communion , according to the Command of Chrift,
" *Mat.* 18. 17. that offences may be prevented and healed, &c.
" *Polit. Ecclef. lib.* 3. *cap.* 16. § 4. *Pag.* 171. 172. Much more he
hath to the fame purpofe in that place, alledging fundry Canons
and Decrees of Synods of reformed Churches, wherein they have
determined that none fhould be received into their Churches, but
by this way of folemne Covenant. And others that have lived a-
mongft them may have been eye-witnesses that this is their ufuall
practife.

Obj. 11. " *But what fhall be faid of the Congregations in* England, *if Churches*
" *muſt be combined by Covenant ? Doth not this doctrine blot out all*
" *thofe Congregations out of the Catalogue of Churches ? For what ever*
" *Covenant may be found in the reformed Churches in other parts , yet it*
" *is plaine that the* Englifh *have none.*

Anfw.   Though we deny not but the Covenant in many of thofe Congregations is more implicite and not fo plaine as were to be defired ; (and what is amiffe in them, in their materialls, or in want of
explicite combining of pure matter, or in any of their wayes, wee
will not take upon us to defend) yet we hope we may fay of them
" with Mafter *Parker, Polit. Ecclef. lib.* 3. *cap.* 16 § 1. *pag.* 167.
" *Non abeſt ea realis & fubftantialis (quanquam magis quàm par erat*
" *implicita) coitio in foedus, eaque voluntaria profeſſio fidei fubftantia-*
" *lis : quâ (Deo gratia) eſſentiam Eccleſiæ idque vifibilis hacufque*
" *fartam tectam in Angliâ confervavit* ; That is, there wants not that
" reall and fubftantiall comming together, (or agreeing in Cove-
" nant, though more implicate then were meete) and that fub-
" ftantiall profeſſion of Faith, which (thanks be to God) hath
" preferved the eſſence of vifible Chuiches in *England* unto this
" day.

     The reafons why wee are loath to fay, that the Congregations
in *England* are utterly without a Covenant, are thefe :

     Fiift, Becaufe there were many Chriftian Churches in *Eng-
land* in the Apoftles time, or within a while after, as Mafter *Fox*
fheweth at large, *Act. & Mon. lib.* 2. beginning *pag.* 137. where
he reporteth out of *Gildas,* that *England* received the Gofpel in the
time of *Tiberius* the Emperour, under whom Chrift fuffered, and
that *Jofeph* of *Arimathea* was fent of *Philip* the Apoftle from *France*
to *England* about the yeare of Chrift. 63. and remained in *England*
all his time, and fo he with his fellowes lay'd the firft foundation
of

of Chriſtian Faith among the Britaine people, and other Preachers and Teachers comming afterward, confirmed the ſame and increaſed it. Alſo the ſaid Maſter *Fox* reporteth out of *Tertullian*, that the Goſpel was diſpearſed abroad by the ſound of the Apoſtles into many Nations, and amongſt the reſt into *Britaine*, yea into the wildeſt places of *Britaine*, which the *Romans* could never attaine unto : and alledgeth alſo out of *Nicephorus*, that *Simon Zelotes* did ſpread the Goſpel to the Weſt Ocean, and brought the ſame into the Iles of *Britaine* : and ſundry other prooſes he there hath for the ſame point. Now if the Goſpel and Chriſtian Religion were brought into *England* in the Apoſtles times, and by their means, it is like that the *Engliſh* Churches were then conſtituted by way of Covenant, becauſe that was the manner of conſtituting Churches in the Apoſtles time, as alſo in the times aſore Chriſt, as hath been ſhewed from the Scripture before in this diſcourſe. And if Chriſtian Congregations in *England* were in thoſe times combined by Covenant, then eternitie of Gods Covenant is ſuch, that it is not the interpoſition of many corruptions that may ariſe in after-times that can diſanull the ſame, except when men wilfully breake Covenant and reject the offers of the Goſpel through obſtinacy, which we perſwade our ſelves they are not come unto : and conſequently the Covenant remaines which hath preſerved the eſſence of Churches to this day ; though the mixture of manifold corruptions, have made the Covenant more implicite then were meete.

Secondly, Becauſe there want no good Records (as may be ſeene in *Seldens Hiſtory of Tithes*) to prove that in former times in *England* it was free for men to pay their Tithes and Oblations where themſelves pleaſed : Now this paying of Tithes was accounted as a dutie of people to their Miniſter, or ſheepe to their Paſtour : and therefore ſeeing this was by their owne voluntary agreement and conſent, their joyning to the Church as members thereof, & to the Miniſtery thereof, as ſheepe of ſuch a mans flock, was alſo by their owne voluntary agreement and conſent : and this doth imply a Covenant It was not the precincts of Pariſhes that did limit men in thoſe dayes, but their owne choice.

Thirdly, Thoſe Queſtions and Anſwers miniſtred at Baptiſme, ſpoken of before, (viz. *Doſt thou renounce ? I doe renounce : doeſt thou beleeve ? I doe beleeve : doeſt thou promiſe ? I doe promiſe*) as they

were ufed in other placcs, fo were they alfo in *England*, and are
unto this day, though not without the mixture of fundry corruptions. Now this doth imply a Covenant. And when the children
came to age, they were not to be admitted to the Lords Supper,
before they had made perfonall Confeffion of their owne Faith,
and ratified the Covenant which was made at their Baptifme by
their Parents, which courfe indeed afterward did grow into a
Sacrament of Confirmation, but that was an abufe of a good Order.

If here it be faid, that the Members of the Parifhionall Affemblies are not brought in by their owne voluntary profeffion, but by
the Authority and Proclamation of the Prince, and therefore they
have no fuch Covenant.

The Anfwer is, that the Chriftian Prince doth but his dutie
when he doth not tollerate within his Dominions any open Idolatry, or the open worfhip of falfe Gods by baptized perfons, but
fuppreffeth the fame : and likewife when he gives free libertie to
the exercife of all the Ordinances of true Religion, according to
the minde of Chrift, with countenance alfo and encouragement
unto all thofe whofe hearts are willingly bent thereunto, *Ezra.* 1.
1. 3. & 7. 13. And therefore this practife of his cannot overthrow
the freeneffe of mens joyning in Church-Communion, becaufe
one dutie cannot oppofe nor contradict another. And fuppofe
that this courfe of the Magiftrate fhou'd feeme to be a forcing of
fome to come in for members who were unfit, (in which cafe it
were not juftifiable) yet this doth not hinder the voluntary fubjection of others, who with all their hearts defired it. When the
Ifraelites departed out of *Ægypt*, there went a mixed multitude
with them, many going with them that were not *Ifraelites* indeed, *Exod.* 12. And in the dayes of *Mordecay* and *Hefther*, many
of the people of the lands became *Jewes*, when the *Jewes* were in
favour and refpect, *Eft.* 8. 17. and fo joyned to them not of their
owne voluntary minde, nor of any fincere heart towards God,
but meerely for the favour or feare of men ; yet this forced or
feined joyning of fome could not hinder thofe that were *Ifraelites*
indeed from being *Ifraelites*, nor make the *Jewes* to be no *Jewes*,
no Church-members.

And the fame may be faid in this cafe, Suppofe the Magiftrates
Proclamation fhould be a caufe, or an occafion rather, of bringing
fome

ſome into the Church, who came not of their owne voluntary
minde, but for feare, or for obteining favour, yet this cannot hinder, but others might voluntarily and freely Covenant to be ſubject to the Goſpel of Chriſt : Such ſubjection and the promiſe of
it being the thing which themſelves did heartily deſire, though the
Magiſtrate ſhould have ſaid nothing in it.

If any ſhall hereupon inferre, that if the Pariſhionall Aſſemblies be Churches, then the members of them may be admitted
to Church priviledges in *New England*, before they joyne to our
Churches : Such one may finde his Anſwer in the Anſwer to the
tenth of the thirty-two Queſtions; Whereunto we doe referre the
Reader for this point. Onely adding this, that this were contrary
to the judgement and practiſe of the Reformed Churches, who
doe not admit a man for member without perſonall profeſſion of
his Faith, and joyning in Covenant, though he had formerly been
a member of a Church in another place, as was ſhewed before out
of Maſter *Parker*.

Laſtly, If any ſay, that if theſe reaſons prove the *Engliſh* Congregations to have ſuch a Covenant as proves them to be Churches, then why may not *Rome*, and the Aſſemblies of Papiſts goe
for true Churches alſo ? For ſome man may thinke that the ſame
things may be ſaid for them that here in Anſwer to this eleventh
Objection are ſaid for the Pariſhes in *England* : Such one muſt remember two things : firſt, that we doe not ſay ſimply, a Covenant makes a company a true Church, but (as was ſaid before)
a Covenant to walke in ſuch wayes of worſhip to God and edification of one another, as the Goſpel of Chriſt requireth. For who
doubts, but there may be an agreement among theeves, *Pro.* 1.
A confederation among Gods enemies, *Pſal.* 83. A conſpiracy
among the *Arabians*, the *Ammonites* and *Aſhdodites*, to hinder the
building of *Hieruſalem*, Neh. 4. 7, 8. And yet none of theſe are
made true Churches by ſuch kind of confederacies or agreements.
And ſo wee may ſay of the Aſſemblies of Papiſts, eſpecially ſince
the Counſell of *Trent*. If there be any agreement or confederacy
among them, it is not to walke in the wayes of the Goſpell, but in
wayes contrary to the fundamentall truths of the Goſpel, as Idolatry in worſhip, Hereſie in doctrine, and other Antichriſtian pollutions and corruptions : and therefore if they combined in theſe
things, ſuch combinations will never prove them true Churches.

The

The Church is the Pillar and ground of truth, 1 *Tim.* 3. 15. But the Religion of Papifts is fo farre from truth, that whofoever liveth and beleeveth according to it, without repentance, cannot be faved. Witneffe their doctrine in the point of vilifying the Scriptures, and in point of free-will, and of Juftification by works, of the Popes Supremacy, of the Sacrifice of the Maffe, of worfhipping of Images, &c. In regard of which, and fuch like, the Holy Ghoft faith, that their Religion is a Sea, *become as the bloud of a dead man, and every foule in that Sea dyeth,* Rev. 16. 3. And therefore agreement in fuch a Religion will never prove them to be true Churches; nor any Affemblies of Arrians, Antitrinitaries, Anabaptifts, or Famelifts, fuppofing them alfo to be combined by Covenant among themfelves.

But now for the Affemblies in *England,* the cafe is farre otherwife; for the Doctrine of the Articles of Religion which they profeffe, and which they promife to hold and obferve (though fome things are amiffe in fome of thofe Articles, and though many perfons live contrary in their lives) yet the doctrine is fuch that whofoever beleeveth, and liveth according to it, fhall undoubtedly be faved, and many thoufands have been faved therein; and therefore Affemblies united by Covenant to obferve this doctrine may be true Churches, when the Affemblies of Papifts and others may be falfe, although they alfo were combined by Covenant: the reafon of the difference rifing from the difference that is in the doctrine and Religion which they feverally profeffe, and by Covenant binde themfelves to obferve, the one being fundamentally corrupt, and confequently pernicious: The other in the fundamentall points Orthodoxall and found.

Secondly, It muft be remembred alfo (which was intimated before) that if fundamentall corruptions be profeffed in with impenitency and obftinacy, then God may difanull the Covenant on his part, and give a Bill of divorce to fuch a people, *Jere.* 3. 8. Now experience and the Scripture alfo doth witneffe of the Jefuited and *Trent*-Papifts, that they repented not of the workes of their hands, of worfhipping Devills, and Idolls of Gold, &c. neither repented they of their murthers, nor of their forceries, nor of their fornications, nor of their thefts, *Rev.* 9. 20, 21.

But now for the Parifh Affemblies in *England,* we hope that we may fafely fay, they doe not finne of obftinacy, but of ignorance,

having

having not been convinced (and many of them never having had means to be convinced) of the corruptions that are amongst them, in respect of their constitution, and worship, and Ministery, and so the Covenant remaining among them, may prove them to be Churches, when it cannot stand the Papists in like stead, they being impenitent and obstinate : Which we doe not speake to justifie the Parishes altogether, as if there were not dangerous corruptions found in them, nay rather (the Lord be mercifull to the sinnes of his people) wee may lament it with teares, that in respect of their members and Ministery, in respect of their worship and walkings, in many of those Assemblies there are found such apparent corruptions, as are justly grievous to a godly soule, that is enlightened to discerne them, and greatly displeasing to the Lord, and indeed had need to be repented of betime, least otherwise the Lord remove the Candlesticke and unchurch them, *Rev.* 2. 5. In a word, the corruptions remaining are just causes of repentance and humiliation : but yet in as much as the Articles of Religion, which they professe, containe such wholesome doctrine, that whosoever beleeveth and walketh according thereunto, in sinceritie, shall undoubtedly be saved, and in as much as the corruptions are not persisted in with obstinacy, therefore wee deny not but they have the truth of Churches remaining.

Obj. 12. " But this opinion of *Church-Covenant*, is holden by none but the " *Brownists*, or those of the *Separation*, and therefore it is not to be re- " ceived.

Answ This ground cannot be made good, that none but they of the Separation are for Church-Covenant, for all the Reformed Churches generally, as was shewed before in Answer to Objection the tenth, are for it in their judgement & practise; and shall all they be condemned for *Brownists, or maintaining unlawfull Separation from the Church? Also Master *Parker* and Doctor *Ames*, men of our owne Nation, famous for holinesse and learning, and moderation, both of them plead for Church-Covenant, and yet neither of them were Brownists, but bare witnesse against that riged Separation. For Doctor *Ames* his judgement of Church-Covenant may " be seene in his *Medulla, Theol. lib.* 1. *cap.* 32. § 14, 15, 17. *Fideles* " *non constituunt Ecclesiam particularem, quamvis simul forsan plures* " *in eodem loco conveniant aut vivant, nisi speciali vinculo intersese con-* " *jungantur, &c.* That is, beleevers doe not make a particular

*By Brownists and Separatists you are to understãd those of the riged Separation.

F ' Church,

" Church, though perhaps there be many of them that meete to-
" gether, and live in the same place, unlesse they be joyned toge-
" ther by some speciall bond amongst themselves : for so one
" Church would many times be dissolved into many, and many
" Churches confounded into one. Now this bond is a Covenant,
" either expressed or implicite, whereby beleevers do binde them-
" selves particularly to performe all such duties, both towards God
" and mutually to one another, as pertaine to the nature of a
" Church, and their edification. And thereupon no man is rightly
" admitted into the Church, but by confession of his Faith, and
" stipulation, or promise of obedience.

These words doe plainely and fully shew his judgement of
Church - Covenant, to be the very same that is held and practised
in *New - England* at this day. And that he was not for that seve-
ritie and rigiditie of separation, may be cleared from sundry of
his workes wherein he plainly and fully beares witnesse against
the same, and namely, in his *Fresh suite against Ceremonies, pag.* 207.
and in his second *Manuduction*, wherein he purposely and at large
dealcs in this Argument of Separation. Sure it is Master *Canne* in
his Booke, wherein he goes about to prove the necessitie of separation from the Non-Conformists principles, doth professedly and
expreslely oppose himselfe against Doctor *Ames* in the point of
Separation, which shewes how farre the good Doctor was from
favouring that way, when they most zealously therein doe count
him to be a speciall opposite of theirs, as indeed he was. And for
Master *Parker*, his judgement of Church-Covenant was heard before in part ; where he so much approveth the practise of the Reformed Churches in this point. And much more may be seene of
his judgement herein, in the sixteenth Chap. of the third booke of
his *Polit. Ecclesiastica*. And yet in the same place, and likewise
lib 1. *cap.* 13. 14. of the same Treatise he plentifully and plainly
shewes his dislike of the wayes of Separation, as is also acknowledged in an Admonition to the Reader, prefixed before that
Booke, by *I. R. suo, suorumque nomine.* So that this Assertion appeares to be untrue, wherein it is said, that *none but Brownists and
Separatists doe approve of Church- Covenant.*

As for the Inference from this ground, that therefore Church-
Covenant should not be received, because it is pleaded for and practised by the Separatists. We Answer, that this will not follow,
                                                              unlesse

unleſſe it could be proved, that the Separatiſts hold no truth; or if they hold a truth wee muſt not hold it, that ſo it may appeare wee differ from them; Either of which, it were unreaſonable to affirme. If the Papiſts hold ſundry Articles of Faith, as that there is a unitie of the Divine Eſſence, and Trinitie of Perſons, that Jeſus Chriſt is God and man, and that true Meſſiah that was promiſed, and the onely Saviour of the world, and many ſuch like, muſt wee deny theſe things becauſe they are holden by the Papiſts? This were as unreaſonable as to condemne the doctrine of the Reſurrection, becauſe it was maintained by the Phariſees, *Act.*23. 8. And ſo we ſay of Church-Covenant, holden and practiſed by them of the Separation; as alſo many other truths are maintained by them : No reaſon that truth ſhould be refuſed, becauſe the Separatiſts maintaine it. When Doctor *Bancroft* in a Sermon at *Pauls*-Croſſe, had avouched that the Superioritie of Biſhops above other Miniſters, is by Gods owne Ordinance, and to make the contrary opinion odious, affirmed that *Aerius* perſiſting in it, was condemned for an Heretique by the generall conſent of the whole Church, and that *Martin* and his Companions, doe maintaine the ſame opinion of *Aerius*; What ſaith learned Doctor *Reinolds* hereunto, in a Letter to Sir *Francis Knolls*, who required him
" to ſhew his judgement herein : Touching *Martin*, ſaith he, if
" any man behave himſelfe otherwiſe then in diſcretion and cha-
" ritie he ought, let the blame be laid where the fault is, and de-
" fend him not ; but if by the way he utter a truth , mingled with
" whatſoever elſe , it is not reaſon that that which is of God
" ſhould be condemned for that which is of man : no more then
" the doctrine of the Reſurrection ſhould be reproved, becauſe
" it was maintained and held by the Phariſees : Wherefore remo-
" ving the odious name of *Martin* from that which is ſinceritie
" and love, is to be dealt with, &c.

And the very ſame doe wee ſay to them that would make Church - Covenant to be odious, becauſe it is held by thoſe of the Seperation, who are commonly called Browniſts : If men behave themſelves otherwiſe then they ought, we defend them not therein, but if they hold any truth mingled with whatſoever elſe , wee would not have that which is of God to be condemned, for that which is of man : truth ſhould not be refuſed , becauſe of other corruptions that may be found in them that hold it.

Reply.   " *If you with them hold Church-Covenant, you iustifie them in all*
            " *their Wayes of seperation and erronious opinions.*

Answ.   Not so, for many of them hold that there are no visible Chri-
            stians that stand members of the Parishes in England, and that it
            is not lawfull to hold any private Religious communion with
            such persons; and that the parishionall Assemblies are none of
            them true Churches, and that it is not lawfull to hear any of those
            Ministers to preach the Word, none of which are justified at all
            by holding Church-Covenant, though they do hold the same;
            There is no such necessarie and inseparable connexion betweene
            these opinions, and that of Church-Covenant, that he that holds
            this, must needs hold the other also.

Obje.13.   " *But the time hath been, when your selves did not hold Church-Co-*
            " *venant, as now you do; when you were in England you were not of this*
            " *mind, and therefore no marvell if your change since your coming to New*
            " *England be suspected, and offensive. If you change your judgement*
            " *and practise in this manner, God knows whether you may come at last,*
            " *and therefore men may well be afraid of holding with you in this point,*
            " *which your selves did not hold when you lived in your native Countrey.*

Answ.   Some of us when we were in *England*, through the mercie of
            God, did see the necessitie of Church-Covenant; and did also
            preach it to the people amongst whom we ministred, though nei-
            ther so soone nor so fully as were meete, for which we have cause
            to be humbled, and to judge our selves before the Lord.

            But suppose we had never knowne nor practised the same be-
            fore our coming into this countrey, yet if it be a truth of God,
            there is no reason why we should shut our eyes against the light,
            when God holds it forth unto us, nor that others should be offend-
            ed at us for receiving the same. For by the same reason men
            might still continue in their sinnes, and not make any progresse
            in knowledge and holinesse, that so they may not seeme uncon-
            stant, which were contrary to the Scripture, wherein we are com-
            manded not to fashion our selves according to the former lusts of
            our ignorance. 1. *Pet.* 1. 14. But to be changed, *Rom.* 12. 2. and
            renued, *Ephes.* 4. 23. and put off the old man, and put on the new,
            Ephes. 4. yea to grow in grace and holinesse, 2. *Pet.* 3. 18. and be
            stronger and stronger, *Job* 17. 9. that our good workes may be
            more at the last, then at the first, *Revel.* 2. 19. Sure it is, the Apo-
            stle tells the *Corinthians* and *Ephesians*, that the time had been
                                                                    when

when they were not the same men that now they are when he wrote unto them ; and yet he doth not blame them for leaving their former opinions or practise, but commends them for it, 1. *Cor. 6. 11. Ephes. 2. 3.* &c. And it is said of *Apollos* an eloquent man, and mighty in the Scripture. that when he came to *Ephesus* the way of God was expounded unto him more perfectly by *Aquila* and *Priscilla*, whereas before he was instructed in the way of the Lord, knowing onely the Baptisme of *John* : yet this was no dispraise at all to him, that now upon better information he would change his judgement to the better, nor unto them that were the means thereof : *Act. 18. 25, 26. Nullus pudor est ad maliora transire.*

The time hath been, (and we may be humbled for it) when we lived without God in the world, and some of us in many sinfull courses : and shall any be offended, because we are not still the same ? and when God called us from the wayes of sin and death, to the Fellowship of his grace in Christ; yet some of us lived a long time in conformity to the ceremonies imposed in our native Countrey, and saw not the evill of them. But when God did open our eyes, and let us see the unlawfulnesse thereof, we cannot see but it would have been a with-holding the truth in unrighteousnesse, and a great unthankfulnesse to God for light revealed to us, if we should still have continued in that course through an inordinate desire of seeming constant : and therefore it is not any just cause of offence that we have changed our judgement and practise in those things, when we once perceived the Word of God to disallow them.

Indeed it hath been sometime objected against Mr. *Cartwright*, and others, that desired the reformation of the Churches in *England*, in regard of Discipline and Church-Order, that they which stood so much for Reformation in Discipline, did in after times adde and alter some things, beyond what they saw at first, and what themselves had formerly desired ; and that therefore being so mutable, and inconstant in their apprehensions, they were not to be regarded, nor hearkened unto : to which Objection Mr. *Parker* makes full Answer *in Ecclef. lib. 2. ca. 36. p. 307.* where he sheweth from the Scripture, and the testimonie of Bishop *Jewel*, " Doctor *Reinolds*, and others, that in the Reformation of Reli- " gion God brings not his servants into perfection in knowledge " and zeale at the first, but by degrees, so as they grow and make

F 3   " progresse

" progresse in these things in such wise, that their good works are
" more at the last then at the first, as was said of the Church of
" *Thyatira*, even as the man that had been blind, when Christ re-
" stored him to his sight, could at the first but see men like trees
" walking, and afterward saw every man cleerly; and therefore it
" is no good arguing to say these men have altered and corrected
" such things from what their apprehensions were at first, and
" therefore they are not to be regarded.

Now if this be no good arguing against Mr. *Cartwright*, and
those that in *England* have been studious of Reformation (as indeed it is not) then it is no good Argument against us in this matter of Church-Covenant, to say we now hold and practise otherwise then we have done in former time.

Reply.   " *If any shall here reply, that change from conformity to the ceremo-*
" *nies to Worship God more purely is warranted by the Word, and there-*
" *fore not blame-worthy, and that the same may be said of the case of*
" *Apollos, of the Corinthians, and Ephesians forementioned, and of* Cart-
" wright, *and the rest in his times.*

Answ.   We answer, that this is true, and thereby it appears, that it is not
simply the changing a mans opinion or practise that can be counted blame-worthy, or offensive, but changing without warrant of
the Word; and therefore in point of Church-Covenant, the issue
must not be whether we or others have formerly known and practised it, but whether it have ground from Gods Word; For if it
have (as we hope have been proved before in this discourse) then
the observing of it, can be no cause of just offence unto others, nor
imputation of inconstancy to our selves, though in time past we
had not had so much light as to discerne the necessitie and use
thereof.

The good Lord pardon every one that prepareth his heart to
seek God, though he be not cleansed according to the purification
of the Sanctuary: and grant unto all his Churches and servants,
that their love may abound yet more and more in knowledge, and
in all judgement, that they may discerne the things that differ;
and approve the things that are excellent, and by his Spirit of
truth be led forward into all truth, till Antichrist be utterly consumed with the breath of his mouth, and the brightnesse of his
coming, and the holy City new Jerusalem come down from God
out of heaven, as a Bride adorned for her husband the Lambe, the
Lord Jesus, to whom be all glory of affiance and service for ever
Amen.   *F I N I S.*

AN
ANSVVER
OF THE ELDERS
OF THE SEVERALL
CHVRCHES IN
NEW-ENGLAND
unto Nine POSITIONS,

SENT OVER TO THEM
(By divers Reverend and godly Mi-
nisters in ENGLAND) to declare their
Judgements therein.

Written in the Yeer, 1639.
And now published for the satisfaction
of all who desire resolution in those points.

LONDON,
Printed by *T. P.* and *M. S.* for *Benjamin Allen.*
1643.

The severall *Positions* handled in this Treatise.

1. THat a *stinted Forme of Prayer, or set Liturgie,* is unlawfull.

2. That it is not lawfull to joyne in Prayers, or receive the Sacrament where a stinted Liturgie is used, or as we conceive your meaning to be in this as in the former Question, viz. where that stinted Liturgie is used.

3. That the children of godly and approved Christians, are not to be baptised untill their parents be set members of a Congregation.

4. That the parents of themselves though of approved piety, are not to be received to the Lords Supper, untill they be admitted as set Members.

5. That the power of Excommunication, &c. is so in the Bodie of the Church, that what the major part shall allow, that must be done, though the Pastors and Governors, and part of their Assembly be of another mind, and peradventure upon more substantiall Reasons.

6. That none are to be admitted as set Members, but they must promise not to depart or remove, unlesse the Congregation will give leave.

7. That a Minister is so a Minister to a particular Congregation, that if they dislike him unjustly, or leave him, he ceaseth to be a Minister.

8. That a Minister cannot perform any ministeriall Act in another Congregation.

9. That Members in one Congregation may not communicate in another.

AN

AN EPISTLE WRITTEN
by the *Elders* of the Churches in
NEW-ENGLAND, to thofe godly
Minifters forementioned that fent
over the POSITIONS.

Reverend and beloved Brethren :

IN thefe remote Coafts of the earth, whereunto the good hand of God hath brought us, as we do with much comfort of heart call to mind the many gracious bleffings, which both with you, and from you we injoyed in our Chriftian and holy communion, (the memory and fruit whereof we hope fhall never be blotted out) fo we have alfo feene caufe to look back to our former adminiftrations there, and to fearch and trie our wayes; that wherein foever we have formerly gone aftray, we might judge our felves for it before the Lord : And that feeing now God hath fet before us an open doore of libertie, we might neither abufe our libertie in the Gofpel, to runne out into any groundleffe unwarrantable courfes, nor neglect the prefent opportunitie to adminifter (by the help of Chrift) all the holy ordinances of God, according to the patterne fet before us in the Scripture; In our native Countrey, when we were firft called to the Miniftery, many of us took fome things to be indifferent and lawfull, which in after times we faw to be finfull, and durft not to continue in the practife of them there; Afterwards fome things that we bare as burthens, that is, as things inexpedient, though not utterly unlawfull; we had no caufe to retain and practife the fame things here, which would not have been not onely inexpedient, but unlawfull: fuch things as a man may tollerate when he cannot remove them, he cannot tollerate without finne when he may remove them; Befides fome things we practifed there (which we fpeake it to our fhame and griefe)

we

we never took it into serious consideration whether they were
lawfull, and expedient or no, but took them for granted, and generally received; not onely by the most Reformed Churches, but
by the most godly and judicious servants of God amongst them;
which neverthelesse when we came to weigh them in the ballance
of the Sanctuarie, we could not find sufficient warrant in the
Word to receive them, and establish them here: of one of these
three kinds will these our present practises appeare to be, which
you call our new opinions, or, Innovations here; except it be
some few of them, which though they have been reported to you
to be our Judgements and practises, yet are indeed farre from us:
The particulars are too many, and too weightie to give you account of them, and the ground of our proceedings about them
in a Letter. But to give you (if it be the will of God) the better satisfaction, we have sent you a short Treatise touching each particular, that according to your desire you might understand from
us how farre we do acknowledge any of these tenents, and upon
what ground hoping that according to your promise, if upon due
examination you shall find any weight in them, you will give us
the right hand of fellowship. But if otherwise, you will send us
your just and faithfull animadversions, and we do not suspect your
loves to the truth, or your sincere speaking according to your
conscience in the sight of God, neither taxe you as a side from the
truth with by respects, whereof you complaine, verily we abhorre
such rash, harsh, and presumptuous notoriousnesse; we see as
much cause to suspect the integritie of our own hearts, as yours;
and so much the more, as being more privie to the deceitfulnesse
of our own hearts then to yours. And we cannot but with much
thankfulnesse of heart acknowledge the many rich precious trea-
sures of his grace, wherewith the Lord hath furnished sundrie of
you above your Brethren, which causeth us with great reverence
to accept, and receive what further light God may be pleased to
impart unto us by you; But as we have beleeved, so have we hitherto practised, and so have most of us spoken: this our Answer
to your particulars, most of us we may say, because there wants
not some Brethren amongst us who proceed further, even to look
at all set formes of Prayer invented by men of another age or
congregation, and prescribed to their Brethren to be read out of a
book for the prayers of the Church, as Images, or Imaginations
                                                            of

of men, forbidden in the ſecond Commandement. But as we leave them to their libertie of their own judgements without pre-judice, ſo do we alſo concurre with the reſt of them, ſo farre as we all go in bearing witneſſe againſt any ſet formes, or the corrupti-ons in them; In diſpatching whereof, we have been the more ſlow becauſe it behoved us firſt to inquire into, and to ſettle ſome con-troverſies amongſt our ſelves, before we could well attend to en-tertaine diſcourſe about forraigne queſtions which do not ſo neer-ly concerne our preſent eſtate and practiſe. Beſides your Letters being ſent to the Miniſters of the Churches, and ſome of us dwel-ling farre aſunder, it was not an eaſie thing for all of us often to meet together to conſider of theſe Queſtions, much leſſe to reſolve upon one juſt anſwer. But having at length (by the aſſiſtance of God) brought our Anſwers to this iſſue, we commend it to the bleſſing of the Lord, and in him to your Chriſtian, and judicious conſideration; where if all things be found ſafe, and duely war-ranted from Scripture grounds; do you alſo as ſeemeth vigilant Watchmen of the Lords flock, and faithfull witneſſes to God; If any thing ſeeme doubtfull to you, conſider and weigh it very well before you reject it: If any thing appeare to be unſound, and diſſo-nant from the Word (which we for our parts cannot diſcerne) we ſhall willingly attend to what further light God may ſend unto us by you: In the meane while we intreat you in the Lord, not to ſuffer ſuch apprehenſions to lodge in your minds, which you inti-mate in your Letters; As if we here juſtified the wayes of riged ſe-paration, which ſometimes amongſt you we have formerly born witneſſe againſt: and ſo build againe the things we have deſtroy-ed; you know they ſeparate from your Congregations, as no Churches; from the Ordinances diſpenſed by you as meere Anti-chriſtian, and from your ſelves as no viſible Chriſtians. But we profeſſe unfainedly, we ſeparate from the corruptions which we conceive to be left in your Churches, and from ſuch Ordinances adminiſtred therein as we feare are not of God, but of men; And for your ſelves, we are ſo farre from ſeparating as from no viſible Chriſtians, as that you are under God in our hearts (if the Lord would ſuffer it) to live and die together; and we looke at ſundrie of you as men of that eminent growth in Chriſtianitie, that if there be any viſible Chriſtians under heaven amongſt you, are the men which for theſe many yeers have been written in your foreheads (*Holineſſe to the Lord*) which we ſpeak not to prejudice any truth which our ſelves are here taught and called to profeſſe, but we ſtill beleeve though perſonall Chriſtians may be eminent in their growth of Chriſtianitie : yet Churches had ſtill need to grow from apparent defects to puritie ; and from Reformation to Reformation, age after age, till the Lord have utterly aboliſhed Antichriſt with the breath of his mouth, and the brightneſſe of his coming, to the full and cleare revelation of all his holy Truth; eſpecially touching the ordering of his houſe and publick worſhip; as a pledge of this our eſtimation of you, and ſincere affection to you, we have ſent you theſe Anſwers to your demand, and ſhall be readie, by the help of Chriſt, to receive back againe from you, wiſe, and juſt, and holy Advertiſements in the Lord.

Now the Lord God, and Father of our Lord Jeſus Chriſt, your Lord, and ours ; lead us all unto all Truths, purge-out all Leaven out of his Churches, and keep us blameleſſe and harmleſſe in his holy Faith and feare, to his heavenly kingdome, through him that hath loved us ; In whom we reſt,

Your very loving Brethren,
the Elders of the Churches
in New-England.

A N

AN ANSVVER OF THE
Elders of the severall Churches in *New-England*, unto nine *Positions* sent over to them (by divers Reverend and godly Ministers in ENGLAND) to declare their Judgements therein.

POSITION the I.
That a stinted Form of Prayer, or set Liturgie, is unlawfull.

Answ.

BEfore we proceed to declare our selves concerning this Position, it will be needfull that some things be premised for the explication of the termes thereof; we suppose that first (by a Liturgie and forme of Prayer) you meane not a form of private prayer, composed for the helpe of the weaker; but that Siftome, or Body of Publick Prayer, generally used in the English Parishes, comprised for the Churches use by other men, not infallibly guided of God to be said or read out of a book by their Ministers, as the Churches prayers: And that this is your meaning, may appeare from your Letter it self, wherein you complain, that divers in many parts of that Kingdome have lett your Assemblies, because of a stinted Liturgie; now we know not of any other stinted Liturgie from which the people do absent themselves, but onely that which is in use in the English Churches; for as for a Form of Prayer in generall, we conceive your meaning cannot be of that for it is evident that many Preachers constantly use a set form of prayer of their own making before their Sermons, with whom the people refuse not to joyne.

Secondly, by stinted prayers, and set formes, you meane such prayers as are so imposed upon the Churches and Ministers, as that they are limited to the use of that very forme of words exprest in the Book, with no addition, diminution, or alteration; for that Liturgie & Form amongst you is in this sence set & stinted.

Thirdly, by unlawfull, you meane that we looking at that form as swerving from the Rule, neither do first practise it our selves, or

secondly

ſecondly, approve the uſe of it by others.

This being the true ſtate of the Queſtion, ſo far as it appears to us from your Letters, We anſwer:

1. For our own practiſe the Churches here do not uſe any ſtinted form of Prayers, and ſet Liturgies: for theſe and ſuch other like Reaſons.

Firſt, becauſe we find no neceſſitie of a ſtinted Liturgie to be uſed amongſt us, by vertue of any Divine precept; And ſeeing the commiſſion of the Apoſtle limited them to teach men to obſerve and do onely what Chriſt had commanded them in matters of this nature, *Matth.* 28. 20. who are we, and what are our Churches, that we ſhould preſume above this Commiſſion? And we hope it will not be offenſively taken by any godly Brethren, that we ſtand faſt in that Liberty wherewith Chriſt hath made us free, in this as well as in any other thing.

Secondly, becauſe the unlawfulneſſe of ſet Formes, and ſtinted Liturgies, is queſtioned, and doubted of by many faithfull ſervants of Chriſt; whereas for Church Officers to edifie the Church by their own gifts, as well in praying as in preaching, all ſorts without controverſie grant it to be lawfull: Now ſpirituall prudence guideth Beleevers when two wayes are ſet before them, one doubtfull though ventured on by ſome; the other certainly ſafe and good, though neglected by many, to chuſe that which is ſafe, declining from the other.

Thirdly, becauſe the primitive patternes of all the Churches of God in their beſt times, when as touching this point they keep the rule in their eyes; whether Jewiſh before Chriſt, or Chriſtian above an hundred yeers after Chriſt, yeeld not the leaſt foot ſteps to ſhew us another ſafe way to walke in, then this which we have choſen. As for after times towards the end of the ſecond and beginning of the third Century, we know how farre the Churches were then degenerated, and declined from their firſt puritie; nor do we marvell at it, ſeeing in the Apoſtles time the myſtery of iniquitie began to work, and it was then foretold, that the power of godlineſſe would in after times be exchanged for empty forms; in which reſpect we look not at them as our guides, neither in this or other particulars; nor warranted by the Rule: herein following the adviſe of *Cyprian*, who himſelfe ſaw the corruptions of thoſe times, *Non eſt attendendum quid aliquis ante nos faciendum putaverit,*

taverit, sed quid qui ante omnes est Christ: fecerit & faciendum prae-eperit. To conclude, seeing our Christian liberty frees us from binding our selves to any religious observances, whereunto the written Word doth not bind us ; And seeing spirituall prudence directs us to chuse those wayes which on all hands are confessed to be safe, avoiding those that are doubtfull and hazardous, and seeing it will not be safe for us needlesly to swerve from the constant practise of all Churches that are recorded in the Scriptures, that held forth as a cloud of witnesses for us to follow in matters of this nature; we therefore, may not, do not, dare not, use that forme of prayer, and stinted Liturgie in those Churches ; more particularly in that we do not use that Forme of Prayer and stinted Liturgie which is in use among your selves : this and such other like Reasons have induced us thereunto.

First, the many and just exceptions whereunto that Liturgie is liable for matter and manner : for the proofe whereof, we referre you to those servants of God who have gone before us in witnessing against the same ; amongst others, to Dr. *Cartwright*, and the Abridgement.

Secondly, In as much as that Liturgie was never commanded of God, and hath been greatly abused to idolatry and superstition, and is not of any necessarie use, therefore we are afraid to bring it into the worship of God, as knowing (*Exod.* 20.) the jealousie of the Lord in matters of this nature, and how strictly he commanded his people, that all monuments of Idolatrie and superstition should be abolished from among them : *Deut.* 5.25,26. *Exod.* 13. *Isa.* 30. 32. 2. *Cor.* 6. 17: in which respect the holy Ghost hath greatly commended *Jacob, David, Jehu, Hezekia,* and *Josia,* for taking away the remembrance of such things, (*Gen.* 33.24. *Psal.* 6. 4. 2. *King.* 20. 26, 27. 18. 4. 2. *King.* 23. all the Chap.) and when other Kings of *Judah,* came short of the same zeale, the Scripture notes it as a blemish in them, that the high places were not taken away, albeit the people did not sacrifice in them to false gods, but onely to the Lord, 2. *Chron.* 15. 17. and 20. 32. and 32. 17 yea moreover it appeareth by the Scripture that some things that had a good originall and use, if they be not still necessarie and commanded of God, are unlawfull, when once they are known to be defiled by Idolatrie, and abused to it, 1. *King.* 18. 14. *Hos.* 2. 16. 17. As the brazen Serpent was at the first Gods institution, though but temporarie, but when the children of Israel burnt incenfe to it, *Hezekiah* is commended for breaking it in peeces: and the Lord witneffed of him, that herein *he did that which was right in the fight of the Lord, and according to his Commandements which he commanded Mofes.* 2. King. 18. 3. 46. How much more in the like cafe ought other things to be removed which never were commanded of God, but onely were devifed by men; And that that Liturgie hath been fuperftitioufly abufed, may be cleare to any that fhall confider. It is the fame for fubftance that was ufed in the dayes of Poperie; and therefore when the Papifts in *Devon-fhire*, and *Cornwell* had made a commotion and Rebellion upon the change of Religion in the dayes of King *Edward* the fixth, it was told then by the King, for the pacifying of them, that it was the felf-fame fervice in Englifh which had been before in Latine, (it remaineth good in Englifh, for nothing is altered) And Pope *Pius* the fifth did fee fo little variation in it from the Latine Ser-vice, that had been formerly ufed in that Kingdome, that he would have ratified it by his Authoritie, if Queene *Elizabeth* would have fo retained it: And many of the people put fuch holineffe in it; that they thinke God is not rightly worfhipped, nor the Sabbath obferved, nor the Sacraments fufficiently adminiftred, if there be no reading of the Service. And others put fuch holineffe and ne-ceffitie in it, that they preferre it before Gods holy ordinances of preaching the Word, in fo much as the Minifters are in danger of being called into queftion, and of being cenfured, if they do not read the Liturgie every Lords day, without omitting any part thereof, either in refpect of preaching, or other wayes: This Ar-gument is ufed in the abridgement, againft Conformitie to the Ceremonies, and we do not fee but it is as ftrong againft the Li-turgie.

Thirdly, In regard of the many wofull fcandalls and dangerous confequences of ufing that Liturgie, of which, wee fuppofe, you are not ignorant: to mention but two; firft, the hardening of Papifts, who are imboldened to thinke better of their owne Bre-viaries, and Maffe-Bookes, feeing moft of that Liturgie hath been extracted out of thefe Bookes, and rather fetched from them, then from the formes ufed in any parts of the reformed Churches; Secondly, The countenancing and eftablifhing of an unlearned Idoll-Miniftery, of not-Preaching-Curates, Non-refidents, Plu-ralifts,

ralifts, &c. In whofe skirts is to be found the bloud of fo many thoufand foules, living and dying in their finnes, whileft they ignorantly content themfelves with, and harden themfelves in fome emptie formes of Religion, and blinde devotion, which are begot and cherifhed chiefly by fuch Prayers and Miniftery : Neither is there leffe fcandall thereby (we meane) not onely taken but given them, by the eating of an Idolethite in the Idolls Temple, condemned by the Apoftle, 1 *Cor.* 8. 7. 10. For if the eating of an Idolethite by him that had knowledge, and knew that an Idoll was nothing, and that all meats were lawfull, did imbolden others to honour the Idoll, and therefore was a fcandall given, fo alfo is it in this cafe.

Fourthly, Seeing that Booke is fo impofed, as that the Minifter in reading of it, is limited to the very words fet downe, without any addition, diminution, or alteration, therefore wee dare not ufe it.

For firft the Lord himfelfe hath not limited his people to his owne forme, therefore wee fee not how it can be lawfull for to be limited to other mens formes ; for in thus doing, we fhould fubject our felves to the exercife of fuch an authoritie and power of the Prelates, as in this cafe puts forth a ftronger Act of limiting power then Chrift himfelfe, who doth not limit us to thofe formes which himfelfe hath fet downe in Scripture ; for though wee acknowledge the Lords Prayer, and other formes fet downe in Scripture, may be lawfully ufed as prayers (due cautions being obferved) yet there is not a limitation lying upon the Churches, in the ufe of thefe prayers ; And therefore we doe not finde that the Apoftles ever ufed that forme taught by Chrift in thofe very words, much leffe limited themfelves to it when they prayed ; nor did they teach the Churches fo to doe.

Secondly, If the Lord would not have us limit our felves to our owne formes, whileft we are exercifing our owne gifts, which he hath fpecially fanctified to edifie his Churches, *Act.* 6. 4. *Eph.* 4:8. 1 *Cor.* 12. 17. Leaft wee fhould quench, or at leaft ftraighten his Spirit in prayer, 1 *Thef.* 5. 19. Would he not have us then limited to other mens formes, which have not been in like fort fanctified of God, but will rather quench or ftraighten the Spirit of God, whileft we are fo limited to them.

Thirdly, The entertainment of this forme hath been a manifeft

fnare

snare unto other Churches, who upon the same ground on which they have received this forme into the desire, have been limited to others in the Pulpit, by the means whereof the poore Church of Christ hath been wholly deprived of the publique use of the Ministers gifts in prayer, and the Spirit of prayer in the Ministers in publique hath been greatly restrained.

Secondly, As for our judgements concerning the practise of others, who use this Liturgie in our native Countrey, we have been alwayes unwilling to expresse our minds there against, unlesse wee had been necessarily called thereunto: And at this time we thinke it not expedient to expresse our selves any further concerning this matter, as loath to entermedie in the affaires of other Churches; but contenting our selves with, and blessing the Lord for these Liberties, which wee by the mercy of God doe here enjoy, reserving also due reverence to the judgements of our beloved Countrey men, who concerning this matter may be otherwise minded.

Position the II.

That it is not lawfull to joyne in prayers, or receive the Sacrament, where a stinted Liturgie is used, or as wee conceive your meaning to be in this as in the former question, viz. where that stinted Liturgie is used.

Answ. IT seemes by your Letters, the ground of this your Position hath been the seperation of divers from your Assemblies, because of a stinted Liturgie; And we are not ignorant of that ridged Seperation of divers people, who withdraw themselves from an able faithfull Ministery, as no Ministery of Christ, and from their Congregations, as no Churches of Christ, because of some corruptions, from which through want of light (not love of the truth,) they are not throughly clensed; against which practice we have ever witnessed: As for our judgements concerning the Position it selfe, wee would premise two things:

First, Concerning th persons reading this Liturgie, which may be either an ungodly, or unable Ministery, or an able and godly.

Secondly, Concerning the Liturgie it selfe, which may be understood,

derstood, either of the whole, or some selected prayers, which may be conceived to be the least offensive.

Now if the Question be of joyning in prayer, where and when that whole Liturgie is used, or when that which is used, is read by an unable and ungodly Minister, wee then see not how it can be lawfull to joyne in prayer in such cases; For the prayers of the Minister are not his private prayers, but the publique prayers of the whole Assembly, whose mouth he is unto God ; And when the prayers offered by the Minister, as a living holy acceptable service to God, are not through humane frailtie , but otherwise for matter and manner corrupt, we see not what warrant any man hath to joyne in such prayers, *Act.* 1. 13. 14. When they are joyned therein with an insufficient Ministery, they doe not onely countenance them in their place and office, whom the Lord hath rejected from being his Priests, *Hosea* 4. 6. but also set up those Idolls and *means of worship to edifie themselves by, which God never appointed in his holy Word, *Ezek.* 11. 17

But if the Question be of joyning in some few selected prayers, read by an able and faithfull Minister out of the Booke ; as of the one side wee are tender of imputing sinne to those that so joyne, so on the other side, we are not without feare least such joyning may be found unlawfull ; unlesse it may appeare that the Ministers with whom wee have communion in reading those prayers , doe neither give any scandall, by reading of them , nor give unlawfull honour to a thing abused to Idolatry and superstition, nor doe suffer themselves to be sinfully limited in the reading of them.

* By this Argument all as well as a part of the Common-prayer-Booke, must of necessitie be rejected.

Position the III.
That the children of godly and approved Christians, are not to be Baptized untill their Parents be set members of a Congregation   Position the IV.
That the Parents of themselves though of approved pietie, are not to be received to the Lords Supper, untill they be admitted as set members.

THese two Positions may be maintained with one and the same defence, being somewhat coincident , and therefore wee thus joyne them, as if they were but one.

H 3   First,

First, therefore to prevent all mistakes, it may please you to take notice, that we are not of their judgement, who refuse all religious communion with such as are not Church-members, nor doe wee appropriate in this priviledge of the Seales, onely to the members of our owne Church, excluding all other Churches of Christ from the same, though they may be through error or humane frailtie defective in some matters of order; provided that the libertie of our Churches be preserved, of receiving such satisfaction as is meete, as well by Letters of Recommendation from such Churches, as otherwise; if it be requisite concerning those whom wee admit into fellowship in the Seales, for as wee account it our due tie to keepe the unitie of the Spirit inviolate, with any in whom we descerne any fruits of the Spirit; so we hold our selves bound to discharge this dutie according to our spirituall communion, in prayer, holy conference, and other religious actions of like nature, wee maintaine with all godly persons, though they be not in Church-order: But Church-Communion we hold (with Church-admitting to fellowship of the Seales) the knowne, approved, and orderly recommended member of any true Church; But to fellowship in the Censures admittance of members, and choice of officers, onely the members of that particular Church, whereof they and wee, or any of us stand members.

These things being premised to consideration, whereupon our judgements and practise is swaid; for administration of the Seales onely to such as are members, a priviledge peculiar thereunto in ordinary dispensation, *Rom.* 9. 4. *Act.* 2. 41, 42 47. Indeed the Preaching of the Word is not so, being an Ordinance given not onely for the edifying of the Churches already gathered, but also for the gathering of men to the Church that are yet without, whereas the dispencing of the Seales, are an Ordinance given onely for the edifying of the Church; being ordained, not for the gathering of it; And because there is now no Nationall Church on earth wherein the Seales are dispenced, there being neither place nor time, nor Officers, nor Ordinances appointed in the New Testament by Christ the Lord, for any such Assembly as the *Jewes* had under *Moses*. It remaines that the Christian Churches whereunto these priviledges are given, are Congregationall, consisting onely of so many as may and doe meet together ordinarily in one place, for the publique worship of God, and their edifying. Hence
it is

it is that we reade so much in the New Testament of Churches, in the Plurall number; The Churches of Christ, *Rom.* 16. 6. The Churches of God, 2 *Cor.* 11. 16. The Churches of the Saints, 1 *Cor.* 14. 33. And not onely when they were of divers Nations, the Churches of the Gentiles, *Rom.*16.12. but also of the same Nation, the Churches of Judea, *Gal.* 1. 20. 1 *Thef.* 2. 14. Not onely when the Countrey was of a large circuite and extent, the Churches of Asia, 1 *Cor.*16. 19. but also of a small part of the Countrey, the Churches of Gallatia, *Gal.* 1. 2. Yea, when two Congregations in severall Cities are spoken of, they are called Churches, as the Church of Jerusalem, *Act.* 15. 22. and the Church of Antioch, *Act.* 14. 27. & 15. 25. 30. To winde up all, seeing the Churches under the Gospel, are Congregationall, and that Baptisme and the Lords Supper, belongs onely to the Churches, it will follow that as a Citie priviledge belongeth onely to Citizens and their children; so Baptisme and the Lords Supper, being Church-priviledges, belongs onely to the particular Churches, and their seede, and that seeing *Sigillum sequitur donum*, to apply them to others, what is it but to abuse them ? As a Seale of a Corporation is abused, when added to confirme the Grant of a priviledge which is peculiar to any Towne Corporation, to one that being no freeman of that Corporation is uncapable thereof.

We are not ignorant of what is wont to be objected against *Object.* what hath been said, from Instance of the Centurion, the Eunuch, *Lydia*, the Jaylor, &c. How of the Eunuch no more was required to Baptisme, then beleeving with his whole heart; In the Centurion, the Apostle *Peter* upon his being Baptized with the Spirit, inferred his right to Baptisme with water; So in *Lydia*, the Jaylor, and many others; It being the constant expression of the holy Ghost, *They beleeved, and were Baptized*, without any regard to their Church-Estate.

Whereunto wee Answer; Where the holy Ghost is given and *Answ.* received (which was the case of the Centurion) and where faith is professed according to Gods Ordinance (which was the case of the rest) there none may hinder them from being Baptized, *viz.* by such as have power to Baptize them : In the Instances given, Baptisme was administred, either by Apostles, or Evangelists, or by ordinary Pastours : The persons Baptized, if they were members of Churches, they had a right to Baptisme in their estate;

And

And the Apostles being Officers of all Churches, might dispence the Seales to them where ever they came, which yet will not warrant ordinary Church-Officers to doe the same; nor is it improbable, but that all these were in Church-order. *Aretus* is of opinion in *Act.* 9. 18. *Act.* 8. 37. that the Centurion had a constituted Church in his house; The Eunuch comming to *Jerusalem* to worship, argueth him to be a Proselyte, and member of the Jewish Church, yet dissolved, and therefore upon profession of the Christian faith, capable of Church-priviledges at that time: As for *Lydia* and the Jaylor, it appeareth that in the beginning of the Gospel, there was a Church at *Philippi*, which communicated with *Paul* concerning giving and receiving, and he expressely sayth before his departure from Macedonia, *Phil.* 4. 18. which departure was immediately upon the Jaylors conversion; In which respect what should hinder that *Lydia* and the Jaylor should first be joyned to the Church, & then to be Baptized, though it be not mentioned in that story, as neither is here mention of a Christian Church, which yet *Paul* mentioneth in his Epistle to the *Philippians*, at least it is probable, that *Lydia* was a member of the Jewish Church, because shee is said to be one that worshipped God; But if any man thinke that they were not members of any Church yet Baptized, though we see not how it will be proved, yet if it were so, the objection doth no whit weaken the Argument, which speaketh of the ordinary dispensation of the Seales, and not what was done in an extraordinary way; So that suppose that in the case alledged, Baptisme was dispenced to some that were not in Church-fellowship, yet the example of the Apostles and Evangelists in so doing, will not warrant ordinary Pastours to doe the like.

  The Reason of the difference, why Apostles and Evangelists might administer Baptisme out of Church Orders, whereof Pastors and Teachers may not is double.

1. *Reas.*   First, Because their calling gave them illimited power over all men, especially Christians whereunto they came; But we do not find that ordinarie Pastors and Teachers can do an act of power, but onely over their own Church, which hath called them to watch over them in the Lord.

2. *Reas.*   Secondly, Because they were assisted with an immediate direction and guidance of the holy Ghost, in the particulars of their administrations, in the case alledged; But ordinarie Church Officers
cers

cers are to walke according to the ordinarie Rules of the Scriptures in their dispensation of the seals, and not to expect immediate inspiration, and extraordinarie Revelations for their help in such cases: This difference betweene Apostles and ordinarie Church Officers must needs be acknowledged, or otherwise a man might from their examples justifie Baptisme in private places.

If it be objected, that Baptisme (as Circumcision also former- *Object.*
ly) is a seale of the righteousnesse of faith, and therefore where faith is, and the righteousnesse of it, the seal may be added also, even to those that are not in Church-Covenant by vertue of their relations to the Covenant of grace to all Beleevers. *Rom.* 4. 11.
Gen. 17. 1. to 12.

We answer: The scope of the Apostle in that place of the *Rom. Answ.*
4. is not to define a Sacrament, nor to shew what is the proper adæquate subject of the Sacrament: But to prove by the example of *Abraham* that a sinner is justified before God, not by works, but by faith, (thus) as *Abraham* the Father of the faithfull was justified before God, so must his seed be, that is, all beleevers whether Jews or Gentiles, circumcised or uncircumcised, for therefore *Abraham* received Circumcision which belonged to the Jews to confirme that righteousnesse which he had before, even whilest he was uncircumcised, that he might be the Father of both. But lest any man should thinke his Circumcision needlesse, if he was justified by faith before circumcised, he addeth that his Circumcision was of use, as a seale to confirme to him his faith, and the righteousnesse which is by faith; yet as justification is not the onely thing that Circumcision sealed, but the whole Covenant also made with *Abraham* and his seed was sealed thereby: so *Abraham* is to be considered in using Circumcision, not simply, or onely as a Beleever without Church relation, but as confederate, a beleever, and so in the state and order of a visible Church, though the Apostle maketh mention onely of the righteousnesse of faith as sealed thereby, which was as served for his purpose. Now that circumcision sealed the Church Covenant, may appear from *Gen.* 17. 9, 10, 11. where you may find that *Abraham* & his seed, though beleevers, were not circumcised till God called them into Church-Covenant. There is the same reason and use of Baptisme to us, which serveth to seale to our justification as Circumcision did:

I   yet

yet not that alone, but alſo the whole Covenant with all the priviledges, as Adoption, *Act*. 2. 38. and Sanctification, *Gal*. 3. 26. 27. *Tit*. 3. 5. fellowſhip with Chriſt in his affliction, *Tit*. 3. 5. and the ſalvation of our ſoules ; *Matth*. 10. 23. And the reſurrection of our bodies, 1. *Pet*. 3. 21. And not onely the Covenant of grace which is common to all beleevers, 1. *Corinth*. 15. 29. But Church-Covenant alſo which is peculiar to confederates, according to that of the Apoſtle, *By one Spirit we are all baptiſed into one body*, 1 *Cor*. 2. 13. And by one Body, he meaneth that particular Church of *Corinth*; whereunto he writeth, and ſaith , *Now ye are the body of Chriſt, and members in particular, ver.* 17. And therefore Church memberſhip is required as well to the orderly partaking of Baptiſme, as it was of Circumciſion : nor do we find that Circumciſion was adminiſtred to all that were in the Covenant of grace (as all beleevers were) but onely to ſuch, of them as were joyned to the people of the God of *Abraham*. *Melchiſedech* was under the covenant of grace, ſo was *Lot* , and *Job*, and his foure friends, yet we no where read that they were circumciſed, nor do beleeve they were : ſo that if Circumciſion were adminiſtred to none but thoſe that were joyned to *Abrahams* familie , and the Church of God in his ſeed, then may not Baptiſme in ordinarie courſe be adminiſtred to any beleevers now, unleſſe they be joyned to the Church of Chriſt : For, *Parum par eſt ratio*; But the firſt is true, therefore the ſecond alſo.

Object. If any ſhall ſay, that a man may be a member of a viſible Catholick Church, that ſtands in no relation to any particular Congregation.

Anſw. We anſwer, as we have alreadie ſaid, we know no ſuch Church in the New Teſtament, as a viſible Catholick Church , wherein the ſcales are to be diſpenced: if any man think otherwiſe, and will undertake to prove it from Scripture grounds , we ſhall gladly weigh his Argument, and returne ſuch anſwer as the caſe will beare.

Secondly, the Miniſters of *Scotland* in their examination , and re-examination of the Articles of *Perth*, in the laſt Article touching the adminiſtration of the Sacraments in private places, do expreſſe their Judgements in ſuch termes, as may ſerve for a full anſwer to this Objection.

Viſible communion (ſay they) in the holy things of God is the end

end of our union, and conſolation of a particular Church: becauſe we cannot attaine to viſible communion in the holy things of God immediately, but by our communion with a particular Congregation, this communion muſt not be violated.

The ſecond conſideration, the ordinarie adminiſtration of the ſeales is limited to the Miniſtery, and the Miniſtery to a particular Church; therefore the ſeals alſo muſt neceſſarily be proper to the Church, and to the members thereof.

Thirdly, that the adminiſtration of the ſeals is limited to the Miniſter, is evident from the firſt Inſtitution, where God hath joyned to preach, *viz.* by office, and to baptiſe together; therefore we may not ſeparate them: for howſoever any one man may by the appointment of the Lord, and maſter of the family, ſignifie his mind, and deliver a meſſage from him to the familie, yet the diſpenſing of a fit portion of food to every one of the houſhold, is a branch of the Stewards office. Indeed the keyes are given to the whole Church, yet the exerciſe and diſpenſation of them in this as well as in other particulars is committed to the Miniſters, who are called to be ſtewards of the myſteries of God. 1. *Cor.* 4. 1. And no Church-office can be orderly performed by any but ſuch as are called thereunto; nor will God vouchſafe his preſence and bleſſing whereupon all ſpirituall efficacie depends, in an ordinance, but when it is diſpenſed by ſuch whom he hath ordained and appointed thereunto.

Secondly, that the Miniſter is limited to the Church, appeareth from evident Texts of Scripture, *Act.* 14. 23. ſo alſo upon this ground, 1. *Cor.* 4. 17. 1. *Pet.* 5. 2. *Act.* 20. 28. The office is founded in the relation betweene the Church and the officer: wherefore take away the relation, and the office (and ſo the work) ceaſeth; for where he hath no power, there he may not do any act of power, and he hath no power where he hath no relation by office: herein the proportion holds betweene an Officer of a Towne Corporate, and of a Church, that as the power of the former is onely within his owne corporation; ſo the power of the latter is confined to his own congregation.

The third Conſideration: Circumciſion and the Paſſeover onely are to be adminiſtred to the members of the Church, therefore Baptiſme, and the Lords Supper is to be adminiſtred alſo, &c. The conſequence is made good by the puritie of theſe ordinances: for

if

if the Argument hold ftrong for the proofe of *Pædo-baptifane,* which is taken from the circumcifion of infants, why may we not as well infer a neceffitie of Church memberfhip to baptifme from the neceffitie of it to circumcifion? And that Circumcifion was peculiar to the members of the Church, may appeare in that perfons circumcifed, and they onely might eat the Paffeover, and they might enter into the Temple, which was the priviledge of Church-members.

In our anfwer to the fecond Objection againft the firft Confideration, we have fhewed you that Circumcifion was not adminiftred to all that were under the Covenant of grace, (which all beleevers were) but onely to fuch of them as joyned themfelves to the Church: As firft in *Abrahams* family, whereunto Baptifme doth fo farre anfwer, that the Apoftle accounteth thefe expreffions equivolent: *Col.* 2. 12. to be circumcifed in Chrift with circumcifion made with hands, and to be buried with Chrift in Baptifme, indeed in fome things they differ: as onely the males were circumcifed, whereas alfo with us females are baptifed; the reafon is, becaufe God hath limited circumcifion to the males, but under the Gofpel that difference is taken away.

Againe, Circumcifion was adminiftred in the private familie, but Baptifme onely in the publick Affemblies of the Church. The Reafon of this difference is, becaufe they were bound to circumcife the males on the eighth day, but that would not ftand with going to the Temple, which was too farre off for the people to bring their children from all the parts of *Judea* to be circumcifed on the eighth day: nor had they alwayes opportunitie of a folemne Convention in their Synagogues on every eighth day when fome child or other might be brought to be circumcifed. But there is no precife day fet down for Baptifme; nor are opportunities of publique Affemblies fo remote when Churches are gathered in a congregationall frame; but that every firft day of the week Baptifme may be adminiftred if it be required. Againe for the aforefaid Reafon circumcifion required not a particular Minifter, for ought we find in the Scriptures, but it is not fo in Baptifme, as hath been fhewed in the fecond Confideration: But no good reafon may be given why in this they fhould not both agree, (*viz.*) that they are both to be difpenfed onely to members of the vifible Church, it hath been proved in the firft Confideration.

They

They that are not capable of Church-censures, are not capable 4 *Consid.*
of Church-priviledges ; But they that are not within Church-
Covenant, are not capable of Church-censures ; *Ergo.*

The Proposition is evident ; the Assumption may be proved,
1 *Cor.* 5. 12. *What have I to doe to judge them that are without :* Now
to be without is not onely the case of Heathens, and Excommuni-
cants, but of some beleevers also : who though by internall union
with Christ, they are within the Covenant of grace, yet being
not externally joyned to the visible body of Christ, (a particular
Church) are in regard of a visible Church-communion said to be
without : to this purpose is that Text alledged by other Divines
also, as Doctor *Ames.*

Wee may adde hereunto for a fift Consideration, the evill and 5 *Consi*
pernicious consequences of extending Communion in Church-
priviledges beyond the bond of Church-fellowship : for thus ;

First, the extraordinary office of Apostles, and the ordinary office of Pastours and Teachers, will be much confounded, if the
latter be as illimited as the former in the execution of their office,
beyond the bounds of their owne particular Churches.

Secondly, The second distinction of Church-Assemblies from
the confused multitudes is abrogated ; if without membership in
a particular Church, the Parents may Communicate with the
Church in the Lords Supper, and their seede in Baptisme.

Thirdly, The Church shall indanger the prophaning of the
Seales, and want one speciall means whereby the grace and pietie
of men may be discerned and made knowne, for if without respect to their Church-estate, men of approved pietie, as you say,
are to be admitted to fellowship in the Seales ; how shall their pietie be approved to the Church, not by their owne report of themselves alone, without the attestation of such as are approved by the
Church ? And how can such beare witnes to their approved pietie,
who against light refuse to professe subjection to the Gospel of
Christ, by orderly joyning themselves with fellowship to some
approved Church of Christ, as members thereof, when they have
oppurtunitie thereunto ? Seeing such Church-fellowship is an action of true pietie required of all beleevers in the second Commandement ; and true pietie frameth mens spirits to have respect to
all Gods Commandements ; and we have had much experience of
it ; that men of approved pietie in the judgements of some, have

I 3   been

been found too light, not onely in the judgement of others, but alſo in their owne conſciences, when they have come to the tryall in offering themſelves to be members of Churches: with ſuch a bleſſing hath God followed this Ordinance of taking hold of Church-Covenant, by publique profeſſion of faith and repentance, before men be admitted to the Seales: But this means of diſcovery of mens pietie and ſinceritie, would be wholly left, if men ſhould be admitted to the Lords Table, without entering into Church-fellowſhip.

6 *Conſid.*   None have power to diſpence the Seales but thoſe that are called to the office of the Miniſtery, and no man can be ſo called till firſt there be a Church to call him: Seeing the power of calling Miniſters is given by Chriſt to the Church; and then it followes, that all thoſe who deſired to partake in the Seales, are bound to joyne themſelves together in the Church ſtate, that ſo they may call a Miniſter to diſpence the Seales unto them. And ſeeing this dutie by the appointment of Gods Law, is not onely upon ſome Chriſtians, but equally upon all, therefore no Chriſtian can expect by the appointment of God, to partake in the Seales till he hath joyned himſelfe in Church-fellowſhip, and in the call of the Miniſtery. And indeed ſeeing in a Church, a Miniſter called by the Church, is of ſuch neceſſitie for diſpencing of the Seales, it may ſeeme unreaſonable that Chriſtians ſhould be bound to become a Church, and to call a Miniſter, that ſo the Seales may be diſpenced, and other men (when this is done) may not have equall libertie to the Seals, which refuſe to joyne unto the Church. In conſideration that our practiſe may not be cenſured, as novell and ſingular, give us leave to produce a preſident of the like caſe obſerved and approved by publique Countenance in the dayes of *Edward* the Sixt (of bleſſed and famous memory) who in the yeare 1550. granted *Johannes a Laſco,* a learned Nobleman of *Poland,* and under the Broad Seale of *England,* got libertie to gather a Church of ſtrangers in *London,* and to order themſelves according as they ſhould finde to be according to the Scriptures. Amongſt other godly orders eſtabliſhed in the Church that wch concerned the Adminiſtration of Baptiſme, to prevent the prophaning of it, (wee will report in *Alaſco* his owne words) *Baptiſme in Churches,* ſaith he, *is adminiſtred in the publique Aſſembly of the Church, after the publique Sermon; For ſeeing Baptiſme doth ſo belong to the whole Church, that*

none

none ought to be driven backe which *is a member of the Church, nor to be admitted to it which is not a member of it ; truely it is equall that they should be performed publiquely in the Assembly of the whole Church, which belongeth to the whole Church in common.* Againe he addeth ; *Many seeing our Churches are (by Gods blessing) so established by the Kings Majestie, that they may be, as it were, a Parish of strangers, dispersed throughout the Citie, or a body Corporate* (as it is called in the Kings Graunt) *and yet all strangers doe not joyne themselves to our Churches ; yea, there are those whilest they avoyd all Churches, will pretend to the English Church, that they are joyned with us : and to us, that they are joyned to the English Churches, and so doe abuse both them and us ; Least the English Churches and the Ministers thereof should be decceived by the impostures of such men, and that under colour of our Churches, wee doe Baptize their Infants alone, who have joyned themselves to our Churches by publique confession of their Faith, and observation of the Ecclesiasticall discipline. And that our Church may be certaine that the Infants that are to be Baptized, are their seede who have joyned themselves in manner aforesaid, the Father of the Infant to be Baptized (if possible he can) or other men or women of notable credit in the Church, doe offer them to Baptisme, and doe publique professe, that it is the seede of the Church, and that wee suffer no strangers to offer Infants to Baptisme in our Churches, who hath not made publique profession of his Faith, and willingly submitted himselfe to the discipline of our Churches ; least otherwise they* who *present the children to Baptisme, might in time plead that they belong to other Churches, and so should deceive the English Churches and their Ministers.*

To those that presented Infants to Baptisme, they propounded three questions ; The first was, *Are these Infants which you offer the seede of our Church, that they may lawfully here be baptized by our Ministery.*

Answer, *Yea* ; This Instance is the more to be regarded, because *Alasco* affirmeth in the Preface to that booke, that this libertie was by the King graunted to them, out of his desire to settle a like reformation in the *English* Churches, which is in effect you see the same with our practise in this particular.

POSITION

Position the V.

That the power of Excommunication, &c. is so in the Bodie of the Church, that what the major part shall allow, that must be done, though the Pastours and Governours, and part of their Assembly be of another minde, and peradventure upon more substantiall Reasons.

Answ. IF the Question had been, whether the power of Excommunication lyes in the body of the Congregation, consisting of Officers and members? Our Answer should be Affirmative, and according hereunto also is our practise, and wee hope your judgements and ours are not different herein; But seeing the Question is, whether it is so in the Body of the Congregation, that what the *Major* part shall allow that must be done, though the Pastours and Governours, and part of the Assembly, doe dissent upon more substantiall Reasons.

Our Answer is Negative, *viz.* that the power of Excommunication is not sealed in the Congregation, neither ought it to be in any of the Churches of the Lord Jesus, who ought not to carry matters by number of votes against God, as this Position implyeth, but by strength of rule and reason according to God. The power of the Apostles themselves was not to doe things against truth, but for the truth, 2 *Cor.* 13. 8. and not for destruction, but for edification, 2 *Cor.* 10. 8. And the same may be said concerning the power which God hath given to you, and if any Church amongst us have swarved from this Rule, which is more then we know, we doe not allow them in such a practice, but should be ready as the Lord should help to convince them of their sinne therein.

Position the VI.

That none are to be admitted as set Members, but they must promise not to depart or remove, unlesse the Congregation will give leave.

OUr Answer hereunto is briefly this, Wee judge it were expedient, and most according to Rule, that such Brethren as are in Covenant with the Church, and our selves as fellow-members, and

and have committed their soules to us as Ministers, should not forsake our fellowship, nor abruptly breake away from us, when, and whether they please : But first approve themselves therein to their brethrens consciences, and their counsell in so weightie a matter : For which wee propound to your consideration these two Reasons following.

The former is drawne from the nature of the Church-Covenant, and confession in these foure particulars.   1. *Reas.*

First, Every member at his admission doth openly professe, and solemnly promise, that by Christs helpe assisting, he will not onely in generall give up himselfe as to the Lord, to be guided by him, so to the Church according to God, to be directed by them (which is no more then the members of the Church of *Macedonia* did, 2 *Cor.* 8. 5. in a paralleli case) but also in particulars, that he will performe all duties of Brotherly love and faithfulnesse to all the members of the Body, as of diligent watchfulnesse over all his brethren, throughly to prevent sinne ; so of faithfull admonition after their falls, to regaine them to the Lord from their sinne : therefore men are injoyned hereunto, & that deeply condemned in *Cain* that he would not doe that dutie of being his Brothers keeper, *Levit.* 19 17. and by Christ himselfe, *Mat.* 18. 15. and by *Paul* also, *Gal.* 6. 1.

Secondly, Those ingagements named, are not made onely by the members admitted to the Church, but by the Church backe againe to the members ; So that thereby the whole Church in generall, and every member in particular, stands as well in conscience bound to performe all duties of love and watchfulnesse to him, as he doth to them. And this wee doe according to the golden Rule of love and equitie enjoyned by our Saviour, *Mat.* 7. 12. fearing the contrary practise of Scribes and Pharisees, so much condemned by Christ, of laying greater burdens on o hers then we our selves are willing to undergoe, *Mat.* 23. 4.

Thirdly, These promises they are lawfully and mutually made, that members (as also the whole Church) are bound not onely every one for himselfe actually to performe them, but passively also to suffer his Brethren to doe these offices upon and towards himselfe ; if he neglect his former, he shall falsifie his Covenant, before God, Angells, and men made, and so not onely breake promise to his Brethren, contrary to *Psal.* 15. 4. but also in some sort commit

K   the

the sinne of *Ananias* and *Saphira*, in lying to the holy Ghost, condemned and punished secretly by Gods own hand, *Act.* 5. 3. 10. If he failes in the latter, he shall not onely be guiltie of the same sinne of the breach of Covenant with God and man, as in the former, but shall adde unto it this folly of despising counsell so much commended, *Prov.* 12. 15. 1. 7. And shall also proclaime this his foly and pride, by shewing to all the Church that he *is* wise in his own eyes, and leane unto his own wisedome, both reproved, *Prov.* 3. 7. 13. 4. Seeing need of no further light to be held forth by his brethren, then what he apprehends himself, which is one of the greatest properties of folly it self.

From all these things premised, it appeares we can do no lesse (and yet we do no more) then require a Member before he depart according to our Covenant, thus lawfully, deliberately, and mutually made, to expresse to his Brethren his desire of departing; and the place and societie to which he tends, whether to a godly Church where he may be further edified, or to some corrupt Assembly where he may be destroyed. And secondly, his grounds and Reasons which move him so to do, which if they hold good, being scanned by the Word, he may not onely be confirmed in his way by the consent and advise of many, but counselled also how to manage his departure for his best comfort : and so after all solemnitie with the whole Churches prayers, and blessing in the name of Christ dismissed. But if his grounds be either none at all, or weake, or sinfull, and that his desire of departing savours of self-will, inordinate love of gaine, rash precipitancie, or a spirit of Schisme, more strongly then of sound Reason : Then what can we, what dare we, do lesse without breach of Covenant, then in love and tendernesse, shew him his weaknesse, disswade him from his purpose, and refuse to consent ? Yet if after all this, we see his spirit stedfastly and stiffely bent for a departure, then, though we dare not act against our light by consenting or counselling, yet if his sinne be apparent, and danger eminent, we use rather through Indulgence (in cases of like nature) to suspend our Vote against him, as not willing against his will to detaine him, abhorring to make our Churches places of Restraint and imprisonment.

Object.

But if any man should object, that this Argument holds firme, where this our Church-Covenant is allowed to be lawfull, but with some it is questioned.

Some

Some indeed have queſtioned the neceſſitie of the Church-Covenant, but we hope our Reverend Brethren that we write unto do not queſtion the lawfulneſſe of ſuch a Covenant, being nothing elſe for the matter of it, but a promiſe of doing ſuch Chriſtian duties, as the Goſpel of Chriſt requires of all Saints in Church ſtate : For as we do not hereby promiſe to performe any new duty to our Brethren which was not before commanded us of the Lord, but onely review and renew our purpoſe afreſh, performing ſuch duties to that particular Body into which we are there to be incorporated, as were before injoyned in the Word ; as to love each other, and to watch over each other (out of love) for their good, to be readie to give counſell to, and take counſell from each other, to prevent ſinne in them, or gaine them from ſin, all which are plentifully and frequently held forth in the Scriptures : for the defect of which care and watchfulneſſe, all the Body ſhall be wrapped in the ſame guilt and puniſhment with the members that commit the ſinne, as the whole Church of Iſrael was in *Achans* ſin and puniſhment.

Secondly, Its a thing very ſeaſonable, and a knowne fundamentall rule in all Societies, that he that is incorporate thereunto, and ſo participates of the priviledges thereof, ſhould ingage himſelfe to conforme to all ſuch lawfull rights and orders as are expedient for the well being of the Society, the contrary whereunto will be a thing injurious to him to offer, and confuſion to themſelves to accept.

A ſecond Ground, is drawne from the neceſſarie Ruine that may fall upon the Body, if every particular member ſhould depart at his own pleaſure ; for as every Societie, ſo much more a Church of Saints, both from principles of Nature, and Chriſtianity alſo, not onely lawfully may, but in duty are bound, to indeavour the preſervation of it ſelf : And therefore timely to foreſee, and wiſely to prevent all ſuch things, as would bring deſtruction to it ſelf. Now if any member might when and wherefore he pleaſe, without conſent of the Church depart away from it, this may by unavoidable conſequence deſtroy the whole : For if one man may ſo depart, why may not another alſo, though never ſo uſefull in that Body, whoſe abſence might much change the well being of it, and if one, why not 2. 6. 10. 12. as well as one ? for where will you ſtop, ſeeing all may plead the ſame libertie ? and if members

may

may ſo do, why may not the Paſtor and Teacher alſo, ſeeing they are tyed to him by the ſame relation that he is to them ? And ſo the principall falling, the whole building muſt fall down. And if that may be ſo in one Church, why not in all? and ſo Chriſt ſhould have no certain ſetled Church on earth.

POSITION the VII.

That a Miniſter is ſo a Miniſter to a particular Congregation, that if they diſlike him unjuſtly, or leave him, he ceaſeth to be a Miniſter.

OVr Anſwer to this conſiſts in two branches. Firſt, in caſe a Miniſter be ſet aſide by the Church, meerly through his own default. Secondly, by the Churches fault, without any deſert of his. In the former caſe, it is evident he ceaſeth to be a Miniſter to them any longer, as appeares in foure concluſions.

Firſt, It is cleare from the Word, that a Paſtor, or a Teacher in theſe dayes hath no Apoſtolicall power over all Churches, but onely limited to that one Church where God hath ſet him. *Paul* gives the Elders at *Epheſus* not a generall commiſſion to go to teach all Churches, but to feed one flock, in which the holy Ghoſt hath made them Over-ſeers. *Act.* 20. 28. So *Peter* gives direction to Elders, to feed that flock of God onely which was amongſt them, and to take the over-ſight thereof. 1. *Pet.* 5. 2.

Secondly, It is as cleare, that all this power of feeding which the Miniſter hath in that church, is nextly derived to him from Chriſt, by the Church who hath ſolemnly called him to the worke, and promiſed to obey him therein ; for if he hath it elſe-where, it muſt be either from Chriſt himſelf immediately, or from ſome others deputed by Chriſt to conferre it on him; or he muſt take it up him-ſelfe. Not the firſt, for that was proper to the Apoſtles, or Apoſtolicall men : therefore *Paul* proving his Apoſtleſhip, ſaith, he *was called not of men, nor by men, but by Jeſus Chriſt himſelfe,* Gal. 1. 1. Not the ſecond, for we never read in Gods Word of any ordinarie Officers, or others beſides the Church, that had any Commiſſion given them from Chriſt to call Miniſters unto Churches;

No

Not the third, for no man taketh this honour, (*viz.*) of a Prieſt, but he that is called of God, *Heb*. 5.4. Therefore it muſt needs be from Chriſt by the Church.

Thirdly, as that Church in the name of Chriſt gave this power to a Miniſter, to be what he is, and to do what he doth amongſt them ; when ſuch a Miniſter ſhall make and manifeſt himſelfe apparently unworthy and unfit to diſcharge the place which they thus called him unto ; ſo that they may diſcerne that Chriſt the head of the Church hath refuſed him, from being a Miniſter unto him; they may then upon as good grounds depoſe him from it, as they called him to it.

Fourthly, when a Church hath thus in Chriſts name put forth this power, of ſhutting, as before they did of opening to a Miniſter, then he muſt ceaſe to be a Miniſter to them any more : For we have no ſuch indeliable character imprinted upon a Miniſter, that he muſt needs be ſo for ever, becauſe he once was ſo : his miniſtery ceaſing, the Miniſter ceaſeth alſo.

But ſecondly, In caſe the Church ſhall without cauſe, or a ſufficient weightie cauſe, raſhly or wilfully ſet him aſide, whom Chriſt hath ſet over them; and whom they ſo ſolemnely called, and promiſed before the Lord to ſubmit unto ; and ſo abuſe their power given them by Chriſt : It is doubtleſſe a very great wrong unto the Miniſter, and ſinne againſt Chriſt himſelf, before whom it was done ; and not onely Chriſt himſelfe will take it ill at their hands, for ſuch contempt done to him in his Miniſters (according to Chriſts ſpeech, *Luk.* 10.16. *He that rejecteth you, rejecteth me:* and Gods ſpeech, 1.*Sam.* 8.7. *They have not caſt off thee, but caſt off me.*) But even other Churches alſo may admoniſh them for it; and if they prove obſtinate therein, , withdraw the right hand of fellowſhip from them. And concerning the Miniſter himſelf thus depoſed, ſeeing it is done not by Chriſt, but by the Church without Chriſt, yea againſt the mind of Chriſt, we conceive though he be by them deprived of the execution of his Miniſtery amongſt them, yet untill he accepts of a call to another people, he ſtill remaines a Miniſter of Chriſt, in whoſe account (notwithſtanding ſuch a depoſition) he hath true right of Adminiſtration amongſt the people.

K-3   Poſi-

Position the VIII.

That a Minister cannot perform any ministeriall Act in another Congregation.

Answ. IF you take (ministeriall act) improperly, as sometimes it is taken by some, onely when the Minister of one Church doth exercise his gifts of praying, and preaching in another Church, being by themselves so desired: Then we answer in this sence, a Minister of one Church may do a ministeriall act in another, which he doth not perform by vertue of any office, but onely by his gift. And thus upon any occasion we mutually performe these acts, one in anothers Churches. But if you meane (by ministeriall act) such an act of authoritie, and power in dispensing of Gods ordinance, as a Minister doth perform it to the Church, whereunto he is called to be a Minister; then we deny that he can so perform any ministeriall act, to any other Church but his own; because his office extends no further then his call. For that solemne charge in *Act.* 20. 28. is not to feed all flocks, but that flock onely over which the holy Ghost hath made them over-seers: If that Question were propounded to any Minister, so exercising in another Church, which was once to our Saviour by the chief Priests and Elders [*By what power doost thou these things, and who gave thee this authoritie?*] let that Minister, whosoever he be, study how to make an answer.

Position the IX.

That Members in one Congregation may not communicate in another.

Answ. THis Question (as the other) needs no long Answer, being altogether through misreport mistaken; for members of other Churches well known and approved, by vertue of communion of Churches, do mutually, and without exceptions communicate each of them at others Churches: even so often as Gods providence leads them thereunto, and themselves desire it.

FINIS.

RESEARCH LIBRARY

OF

COLONIAL AMERICANA

An Arno Press Collection

Histories

Acrelius, Israel. **A History of New Sweden;** Or, The Settlements
on the River Delaware . . . Translated with an Introduction
and Notes by William M. Reynolds. Historical Society of
Pennsylvania, MEMOIRS, XI, Philadelphia, 1874.

Belknap, Jeremy. **The History of New Hampshire.** 3 vols., Vol. 1—
Philadelphia, 1784 (Reprinted Boston, 1792), Vol. 2—Boston,
1791, Vol. 3—Boston, 1792.

Browne, Patrick. **The Civil and Natural History of Jamaica.** In
Three Parts . . . London, 1756. Includes 1789 edition
Linnaean index.

[Burke, Edmund]. **An Account of the European Settlements in
America.** In Six Parts . . . London, 1777. Two volumes in one.

Chalmers, George. **An Introduction to the History of the Revolt
of the American Colonies:** Being a Comprehensive View of
Its Origin, Derived From the State Papers Contained in
the Public Offices of Great Britain. London, 1845. Two
volumes in one.

Douglass, William. **A Summary, Historical and Political, of the
First Planting, Progressive Improvements, and Present State
of the British Settlements in North-America.** Boston, 1749–
1752. Two volumes in one.

Edwards, Bryan. **The History, Civil and Commercial, of the
British Colonies in the West Indies.** Dublin, 1793–1794. Two
volumes in one.

Hughes, Griffith. **The Natural History of Barbados.** In Ten Books.
London, 1750.

[Franklin, Benjamin]. **An Historical Review of the Constitution and Government of Pennsylvania, From Its Origin** . . . London, 1759.

Hubbard, William. **A General History of New England, From the Discovery to MDCLXXX.** (*In* Massachusetts Historical Society, COLLECTIONS, Series 2, vol. 5, 6, 1815. Reprinted 1848.)

Hutchinson, Thomas. **The History of the Colony of Massachusetts Bay** . . . 3 vols., Boston, 1764–1828.

Keith, Sir William. **The History of the British Plantations in America** . . . London, 1738.

Long, Edward. **The History of Jamaica:** Or, General Survey of the Antient and Modern State of that Island . . . 3 vols., London, 1774.

Mather, Cotton. **Magnalia Christi Americana;** Or, The Ecclesiastical History of New-England From . . . the Year 1620, Unto the Year . . . 1698. In Seven Books. London, 1702.

Mather, Increase. **A Relation of the Troubles Which Have Hapned in New-England, By Reason of the Indians There From the Year 1614 to the Year 1675** . . . Boston, 1677.

Smith, Samuel. **The History of the Colony of Nova-Caesaria, Or New-Jersey** . . . **to the Year 1721** . . . Burlington, N.J., 1765.

Thomas, Sir Dalby. **An Historical Account of the Rise and Growth of the West-India Collonies,** and of the Great Advantages They are to England, in Respect to Trade. London, 1690.

Trumbull, Benjamin. **A Complete History of Connecticut,** Civil and Ecclesiastical, From the Emigration of Its First Planters, From England, in the Year 1630, to the Year 1764; and to the Close of the Indian Wars . . . New Haven, 1818. Two volumes in one.

Personal Narratives and Promotional Literature

Byrd, William. **The Secret Diary of William Byrd of Westover, 1709–1712,** edited by Louis B. Wright and Marion Tinling. Richmond, Va., 1941.

Byrd, William. **The London Diary (1717–1721) and Other Writings,** edited by Louis B. Wright and Marion Tinling. New York, 1958.

A Genuine Narrative of the Intended Conspiracy of the Negroes at Antigua. Extracted From an Authentic Copy of a Report, Made to the Chief Governor of the Carabee Islands, by the Commissioners, or Judges Appointed to Try the Conspirators. Dublin, 1737.

Gookin, Daniel. **An Historical Account of the Doings and Sufferings of the Christian Indians in New England in the Years 1675, 1676, 1677** . . . (*In* American Antiquarian Society, Worcester, Mass. ARCHAEOLOGIA AMERICANA. TRANSACTIONS AND COLLECTIONS. Cambridge, 1836. vol. 2.)

Gookin, Daniel. **Historical Collections of the Indians in New England.** Of Their Several Nations, Numbers, Customs, Manners, Religion and Government, Before the English Planted There . . . Boston, 1792.

Morton, Thomas. **New English Canaan or New Canaan.** Containing an Abstract of New England, Composed in Three Books . . . Amsterdam, 1637.

Sewall, Samuel. **Diary of Samuel Sewall, 1674–1729.** (*In* Massachusetts Historical Society. COLLECTIONS, 5th Series, V–VII, 1878–1882.) Three volumes.

Virginia: Four Personal Narratives. (Hamor, Ralph. *A True Discourse on the Present Estate of Virginia . . . Till the 18 of June 1614 . . .* London, 1615/Hariot, Thomas. *A Briefe and True Report of the New Found Land of Virginia . . .* London, 1588/Percy, George. *A Trewe Relacyon of the Proceedings and Ocurrentes of Momente Which Have Happened in Virginia From . . . 1609, Until . . . 1612.* (In *Tyler's Quarterly Historical and Genealogical Magazine,* Vol. III, 1922.)/Rolf, John. *Virginia in 1616.* (In *Virginia Historical Register and Literary Advertiser,* Vol. I, No. III, July, 1848.) New York, 1972.

Winthrop, John. **The History of New England From 1630–1649.** Edited by James Savage. Boston, 1825–1826. Two volumes in one.

New England Puritan Tracts of the Seventeenth Century

Cobbett, Thomas. **The Civil Magistrate's Power in Matters of Religion Modestly Debated** . . . London, 1653.

Cotton, John. **The Bloudy Tenent, Washed, and Made White in the Bloud of the Lambe** . . . London, 1647.

Cotton, John. **A Brief Exposition with Practical Observations Upon the Whole Book of Canticles.** London, 1655.

Cotton, John. **Christ the Fountaine of Life:** Or, Sundry Choyce Sermons on Part of the Fift Chapter of the First Epistle of St. John. London, 1651.

Cotton, John. **Two Sermons.** (*Gods Mercie Mixed with His Justice* . . . London, 1641/*The True Constitution of a Particular Visible Church, Proved by Scripture* . . . London, 1642.) New York, 1972.

Eliot, John. **The Christian Commonwealth:** Or, The Civil Policy of the Rising Kingdom of Jesus Christ. London, 1659.

Hooker, Thomas. **The Application of Redemption,** By the Effectual Work of the Word, and Spirit of Christ, for the Bringing Home of Lost Sinners to God. London, 1657.

H[ooker], T[homas]. **The Christian's Two Chiefe Lessons,** Viz. Selfe Deniall, and Selfe Tryall . . . London, 1640.

Hooker, Thomas. **A Survey of the Summe of Church-Discipline** Wherein the Way of the Churches of New England is Warranted Out of the Word, and All Exceptions of Weight, Which Are Made Against It, Answered . . . London, 1648.

Increase Mather Vs. Solomon Stoddard: Two Puritan Tracts. (Mather, Increase. *The Order of the Gospel, Professed and Practised by the Churches of Christ in New-England* . . . Boston, 1700/Stoddard, Solomon. *The Doctrine of Instituted Churches Explained, and Proved From the Word of God.* London, 1700.) New York, 1972.

Mather, Cotton. **Ratio Disciplinae Fratrum Nov-Anglorum.** A Faithful Account of the Discipline Professed and Practised, in the Churches of New England. Boston, 1726.

Mather, Richard. **Church Covenant:** Two Tracts. (*Church-Government and Church-Covenant Discussed, in an Answer to the Elders of the Severall Churches in New-England* . . . London, 1643/*An Apologie of the Churches in New-England for Church-Covenant, Or, A Discourse Touching the Covenant Between God and Men, and Especially Concerning Church-Covenant* . . . London, 1643.) New York, 1972.

The Imperial System

[Blenman, Jonathan]. **Remarks on Several Acts of Parliament Relating More Especially to the Colonies Abroad** . . . London, 1742.

British Imperialism: Three Documents. (Berkeley, George.
*A Proposal for the Better Supplying of Churches in our
Foreign Plantations, and for Converting the Savage
Americans to Christianity by a College to be Erected in the
Summer Islands, Otherwise Called the Isles of Bermuda . . .*
London, 1724/[Fothergill, John]. *Considerations Relative to
the North American Colonies.* London, 1765/*A Letter to a
Member of Parliament Concerning the Naval-Store Bill . . .*
London, 1720.) New York, 1972.

Coke, Roger. **A Discourse of Trade** . . . London, 1670.

[D'Avenant, Charles]. **An Essay Upon the Government of the
English Plantations on the Continent of America** (1701).
An Anonymous Virginian's Proposals for Liberty Under the
British Crown, With Two Memoranda by William Byrd.
Edited by Louis B. Wright. San Marino, Calif., 1945.

Dummer, Jeremiah. **A Defence of the New-England Charters** . . .
London, 1721.

Gee, Joshua. **The Trade and Navigation of Great Britain
Considered:** Shewing that Surest Way for a Nation to
Increase in Riches, is to Prevent the Importation of Such
Foreign Commodities as May Be Rais'd at Home. London,
1729.

[Little, Otis]. **The State of Trade in the Northern Colonies
Considered;** With an Account of Their Produce, and a
Particular Description of Nova Scotia . . . London, 1748.

Tucker, Jos[iah]. **The True Interest of Britain, Set Forth in
Regard to the Colonies:** And the Only Means of Living in
Peace and Harmony With Them, Including Five Different
Plans for Effecting this Desirable Event . . . Philadelphia,
1776.